C-1824   CAREER EXAMINATION SERIES

This is your
PASSBOOK for...

Head Custodian II

**Test Preparation Study Guide
Questions & Answers**

COPYRIGHT NOTICE

This book is SOLELY intended for, is sold ONLY to, and its use is RESTRICTED to individual, bona fide applicants or candidates who qualify by virtue of having seriously filed applications for appropriate license, certificate, professional and/or promotional advancement, higher school matriculation, scholarship, or other legitimate requirements of education and/or governmental authorities.

This book is NOT intended for use, class instruction, tutoring, training, duplication, copying, reprinting, excerption, or adaptation, etc., by:

1) Other publishers
2) Proprietors and/or Instructors of "Coaching" and/or Preparatory Courses
3) Personnel and/or Training Divisions of commercial, industrial, and governmental organizations
4) Schools, colleges, or universities and/or their departments and staffs, including teachers and other personnel
5) Testing Agencies or Bureaus
6) Study groups which seek by the purchase of a single volume to copy and/or duplicate and/or adapt this material for use by the group as a whole without having purchased individual volumes for each of the members of the group
7) Et al.

Such persons would be in violation of appropriate Federal and State statutes.

PROVISION OF LICENSING AGREEMENTS – Recognized educational, commercial, industrial, and governmental institutions and organizations, and others legitimately engaged in educational pursuits, including training, testing, and measurement activities, may address request for a licensing agreement to the copyright owners, who will determine whether, and under what conditions, including fees and charges, the materials in this book may be used them. In other words, a licensing facility exists for the legitimate use of the material in this book on other than an individual basis. However, it is asseverated and affirmed here that the material in this book CANNOT be used without the receipt of the express permission of such a licensing agreement from the Publishers. Inquiries re licensing should be addressed to the company, attention rights and permissions department.

All rights reserved, including the right of reproduction in whole or in part, in any form or by any means, electronic or mechanical, including photocopying, recording, or by any information storage and retrieval system, without permission in writing from the Publisher.

Copyright © 2024 by
National Learning Corporation

212 Michael Drive, Syosset, NY 11791
(516) 921-8888 • www.passbooks.com
E-mail: info@passbooks.com

PUBLISHED IN THE UNITED STATES OF AMERICA

PASSBOOK® SERIES

THE *PASSBOOK® SERIES* has been created to prepare applicants and candidates for the ultimate academic battlefield – the examination room.

At some time in our lives, each and every one of us may be required to take an examination – for validation, matriculation, admission, qualification, registration, certification, or licensure.

Based on the assumption that every applicant or candidate has met the basic formal educational standards, has taken the required number of courses, and read the necessary texts, the *PASSBOOK® SERIES* furnishes the one special preparation which may assure passing with confidence, instead of failing with insecurity. Examination questions – together with answers – are furnished as the basic vehicle for study so that the mysteries of the examination and its compounding difficulties may be eliminated or diminished by a sure method.

This book is meant to help you pass your examination provided that you qualify and are serious in your objective.

The entire field is reviewed through the huge store of content information which is succinctly presented through a provocative and challenging approach – the question-and-answer method.

A climate of success is established by furnishing the correct answers at the end of each test.

You soon learn to recognize types of questions, forms of questions, and patterns of questioning. You may even begin to anticipate expected outcomes.

You perceive that many questions are repeated or adapted so that you can gain acute insights, which may enable you to score many sure points.

You learn how to confront new questions, or types of questions, and to attack them confidently and work out the correct answers.

You note objectives and emphases, and recognize pitfalls and dangers, so that you may make positive educational adjustments.

Moreover, you are kept fully informed in relation to new concepts, methods, practices, and directions in the field.

You discover that you are actually taking the examination all the time: you are preparing for the examination by "taking" an examination, not by reading extraneous and/or supererogatory textbooks.

In short, this PASSBOOK®, used directedly, should be an important factor in helping you to pass your test.

HEAD CUSTODIAN II

DUTIES:
Supervises the cleaning of classrooms and other areas in a school building; orders, stores and issues cleaning supplies; trains newly assigned custodial workers in their duties. Operates and performs maintenance work on electrical, plumbing, heating and ventilating systems including low and high pressure steam boilers and oil burners. Maintains necessary records and prepares required reports relating to personnel, supplies, equipment and work performed. Supervises subordinates. Does related work as required.

SCOPE OF THE EXAMINATION
The written test will be designed to test for knowledge, skills, and/or abilities in such areas as:
1. **Ability to read and follow written instructions** - These questions test for the ability to read, understand and apply written instructions for performing tasks similar to those encountered on the job. All the information needed to answer these questions will be provided in the test booklet.
2. **Building cleaning** - These questions test for knowledge of basic principles and practices of building cleaning. They cover such areas as equipment, tools, supplies, methods and procedures for cleaning different types of surfaces and materials under various, commonly occurring circumstances.
3. **Building operation and maintenance** - These questions test for knowledge of the basic principles, practices and techniques essential to the correct operation and maintenance of public buildings. They cover such areas as building maintenance; preventive maintenance, and minor repair of electrical and plumbing systems; methods and equipment for snow removal; building safety and equipment storage.
4. **Operation and routine maintenance of heating, ventilating and air conditioning systems** These questions test for knowledge of basic principles, practices and techniques essential to the correct operation and maintenance of heating, ventilating and air conditioning systems, including such areas as minor cleaning; room temperature and building ventilation control; steam, hot water and hot air heating systems; boiler operation; troubleshooting air conditioning system problems, and proper maintenance of air conditioning systems.
5. **Supervision and training** - These questions test for the knowledge required by a supervisor to set goals, plan and organize work, train workers in how to do their jobs, and direct workers towards meeting established goals. The supervisory questions cover such areas as assigning and reviewing work, evaluating performance, maintaining work quality, motivating employees, increasing efficiency, and dealing with problems that may arise on the job. The training questions cover such areas as determining the necessity for training, selecting appropriate training methods, and evaluating the effectiveness of training.

HOW TO TAKE A TEST

I. YOU MUST PASS AN EXAMINATION

A. *WHAT EVERY CANDIDATE SHOULD KNOW*

Examination applicants often ask us for help in preparing for the written test. What can I study in advance? What kinds of questions will be asked? How will the test be given? How will the papers be graded?

As an applicant for a civil service examination, you may be wondering about some of these things. Our purpose here is to suggest effective methods of advance study and to describe civil service examinations.

Your chances for success on this examination can be increased if you know how to prepare. Those "pre-examination jitters" can be reduced if you know what to expect. You can even experience an adventure in good citizenship if you know why civil service exams are given.

B. *WHY ARE CIVIL SERVICE EXAMINATIONS GIVEN?*

Civil service examinations are important to you in two ways. As a citizen, you want public jobs filled by employees who know how to do their work. As a job seeker, you want a fair chance to compete for that job on an equal footing with other candidates. The best-known means of accomplishing this two-fold goal is the competitive examination.

Exams are widely publicized throughout the nation. They may be administered for jobs in federal, state, city, municipal, town or village governments or agencies.

Any citizen may apply, with some limitations, such as the age or residence of applicants. Your experience and education may be reviewed to see whether you meet the requirements for the particular examination. When these requirements exist, they are reasonable and applied consistently to all applicants. Thus, a competitive examination may cause you some uneasiness now, but it is your privilege and safeguard.

C. *HOW ARE CIVIL SERVICE EXAMS DEVELOPED?*

Examinations are carefully written by trained technicians who are specialists in the field known as "psychological measurement," in consultation with recognized authorities in the field of work that the test will cover. These experts recommend the subject matter areas or skills to be tested; only those knowledges or skills important to your success on the job are included. The most reliable books and source materials available are used as references. Together, the experts and technicians judge the difficulty level of the questions.

Test technicians know how to phrase questions so that the problem is clearly stated. Their ethics do not permit "trick" or "catch" questions. Questions may have been tried out on sample groups, or subjected to statistical analysis, to determine their usefulness.

Written tests are often used in combination with performance tests, ratings of training and experience, and oral interviews. All of these measures combine to form the best-known means of finding the right person for the right job.

II. HOW TO PASS THE WRITTEN TEST

A. NATURE OF THE EXAMINATION

To prepare intelligently for civil service examinations, you should know how they differ from school examinations you have taken. In school you were assigned certain definite pages to read or subjects to cover. The examination questions were quite detailed and usually emphasized memory. Civil service exams, on the other hand, try to discover your present ability to perform the duties of a position, plus your potentiality to learn these duties. In other words, a civil service exam attempts to predict how successful you will be. Questions cover such a broad area that they cannot be as minute and detailed as school exam questions.

In the public service similar kinds of work, or positions, are grouped together in one "class." This process is known as *position-classification*. All the positions in a class are paid according to the salary range for that class. One class title covers all of these positions, and they are all tested by the same examination.

B. FOUR BASIC STEPS

1) Study the announcement

How, then, can you know what subjects to study? Our best answer is: "Learn as much as possible about the class of positions for which you've applied." The exam will test the knowledge, skills and abilities needed to do the work.

Your most valuable source of information about the position you want is the official exam announcement. This announcement lists the training and experience qualifications. Check these standards and apply only if you come reasonably close to meeting them.

The brief description of the position in the examination announcement offers some clues to the subjects which will be tested. Think about the job itself. Review the duties in your mind. Can you perform them, or are there some in which you are rusty? Fill in the blank spots in your preparation.

Many jurisdictions preview the written test in the exam announcement by including a section called "Knowledge and Abilities Required," "Scope of the Examination," or some similar heading. Here you will find out specifically what fields will be tested.

2) Review your own background

Once you learn in general what the position is all about, and what you need to know to do the work, ask yourself which subjects you already know fairly well and which need improvement. You may wonder whether to concentrate on improving your strong areas or on building some background in your fields of weakness. When the announcement has specified "some knowledge" or "considerable knowledge," or has used adjectives like "beginning principles of…" or "advanced … methods," you can get a clue as to the number and difficulty of questions to be asked in any given field. More questions, and hence broader coverage, would be included for those subjects which are more important in the work. Now weigh your strengths and weaknesses against the job requirements and prepare accordingly.

3) Determine the level of the position

Another way to tell how intensively you should prepare is to understand the level of the job for which you are applying. Is it the entering level? In other words, is this the position in which beginners in a field of work are hired? Or is it an intermediate or advanced level? Sometimes this is indicated by such words as "Junior" or "Senior" in the class title. Other jurisdictions use Roman numerals to designate the level – Clerk I, Clerk II, for example. The word "Supervisor" sometimes appears in the title. If the level is not indicated by the title, check the description of duties. Will you be working under very close supervision, or will you have responsibility for independent decisions in this work?

4) Choose appropriate study materials

Now that you know the subjects to be examined and the relative amount of each subject to be covered, you can choose suitable study materials. For beginning level jobs, or even advanced ones, if you have a pronounced weakness in some aspect of your training, read a modern, standard textbook in that field. Be sure it is up to date and has general coverage. Such books are normally available at your library, and the librarian will be glad to help you locate one. For entry-level positions, questions of appropriate difficulty are chosen – neither highly advanced questions, nor those too simple. Such questions require careful thought but not advanced training.

If the position for which you are applying is technical or advanced, you will read more advanced, specialized material. If you are already familiar with the basic principles of your field, elementary textbooks would waste your time. Concentrate on advanced textbooks and technical periodicals. Think through the concepts and review difficult problems in your field.

These are all general sources. You can get more ideas on your own initiative, following these leads. For example, training manuals and publications of the government agency which employs workers in your field can be useful, particularly for technical and professional positions. A letter or visit to the government department involved may result in more specific study suggestions, and certainly will provide you with a more definite idea of the exact nature of the position you are seeking.

III. KINDS OF TESTS

Tests are used for purposes other than measuring knowledge and ability to perform specified duties. For some positions, it is equally important to test ability to make adjustments to new situations or to profit from training. In others, basic mental abilities not dependent on information are essential. Questions which test these things may not appear as pertinent to the duties of the position as those which test for knowledge and information. Yet they are often highly important parts of a fair examination. For very general questions, it is almost impossible to help you direct your study efforts. What we can do is to point out some of the more common of these general abilities needed in public service positions and describe some typical questions.

1) General information

Broad, general information has been found useful for predicting job success in some kinds of work. This is tested in a variety of ways, from vocabulary lists to questions about current events. Basic background in some field of work, such as sociology or economics, may be sampled in a group of questions. Often these are principles which have become familiar to most persons through exposure rather than through formal training. It is difficult to advise you how to study for these questions; being alert to the world around you is our best suggestion.

2) Verbal ability

An example of an ability needed in many positions is verbal or language ability. Verbal ability is, in brief, the ability to use and understand words. Vocabulary and grammar tests are typical measures of this ability. Reading comprehension or paragraph interpretation questions are common in many kinds of civil service tests. You are given a paragraph of written material and asked to find its central meaning.

3) Numerical ability

Number skills can be tested by the familiar arithmetic problem, by checking paired lists of numbers to see which are alike and which are different, or by interpreting charts and graphs. In the latter test, a graph may be printed in the test booklet which you are asked to use as the basis for answering questions.

4) Observation

A popular test for law-enforcement positions is the observation test. A picture is shown to you for several minutes, then taken away. Questions about the picture test your ability to observe both details and larger elements.

5) Following directions

In many positions in the public service, the employee must be able to carry out written instructions dependably and accurately. You may be given a chart with several columns, each column listing a variety of information. The questions require you to carry out directions involving the information given in the chart.

6) Skills and aptitudes

Performance tests effectively measure some manual skills and aptitudes. When the skill is one in which you are trained, such as typing or shorthand, you can practice. These tests are often very much like those given in business school or high school courses. For many of the other skills and aptitudes, however, no short-time preparation can be made. Skills and abilities natural to you or that you have developed throughout your lifetime are being tested.

Many of the general questions just described provide all the data needed to answer the questions and ask you to use your reasoning ability to find the answers. Your best preparation for these tests, as well as for tests of facts and ideas, is to be at your physical and mental best. You, no doubt, have your own methods of getting into an exam-taking mood and keeping "in shape." The next section lists some ideas on this subject.

IV. KINDS OF QUESTIONS

Only rarely is the "essay" question, which you answer in narrative form, used in civil service tests. Civil service tests are usually of the short-answer type. Full instructions for answering these questions will be given to you at the examination. But in case this is your first experience with short-answer questions and separate answer sheets, here is what you need to know:

1) Multiple-choice Questions

Most popular of the short-answer questions is the "multiple choice" or "best answer" question. It can be used, for example, to test for factual knowledge, ability to solve problems or judgment in meeting situations found at work.

A multiple-choice question is normally one of three types—
- It can begin with an incomplete statement followed by several possible endings. You are to find the one ending which *best* completes the statement, although some of the others may not be entirely wrong.
- It can also be a complete statement in the form of a question which is answered by choosing one of the statements listed.

- It can be in the form of a problem – again you select the best answer.

Here is an example of a multiple-choice question with a discussion which should give you some clues as to the method for choosing the right answer:

When an employee has a complaint about his assignment, the action which will *best* help him overcome his difficulty is to
    A. discuss his difficulty with his coworkers
    B. take the problem to the head of the organization
    C. take the problem to the person who gave him the assignment
    D. say nothing to anyone about his complaint

In answering this question, you should study each of the choices to find which is best. Consider choice "A" – Certainly an employee may discuss his complaint with fellow employees, but no change or improvement can result, and the complaint remains unresolved. Choice "B" is a poor choice since the head of the organization probably does not know what assignment you have been given, and taking your problem to him is known as "going over the head" of the supervisor. The supervisor, or person who made the assignment, is the person who can clarify it or correct any injustice. Choice "C" is, therefore, correct. To say nothing, as in choice "D," is unwise. Supervisors have and interest in knowing the problems employees are facing, and the employee is seeking a solution to his problem.

2) True/False Questions

The "true/false" or "right/wrong" form of question is sometimes used. Here a complete statement is given. Your job is to decide whether the statement is right or wrong.

SAMPLE: A roaming cell-phone call to a nearby city costs less than a non-roaming call to a distant city.

This statement is wrong, or false, since roaming calls are more expensive.
This is not a complete list of all possible question forms, although most of the others are variations of these common types. You will always get complete directions for answering questions. Be sure you understand *how* to mark your answers – ask questions until you do.

V. RECORDING YOUR ANSWERS

Computer terminals are used more and more today for many different kinds of exams.
For an examination with very few applicants, you may be told to record your answers in the test booklet itself. Separate answer sheets are much more common. If this separate answer sheet is to be scored by machine – and this is often the case – it is highly important that you mark your answers correctly in order to get credit.
An electronic scoring machine is often used in civil service offices because of the speed with which papers can be scored. Machine-scored answer sheets must be marked with a pencil, which will be given to you. This pencil has a high graphite content which responds to the electronic scoring machine. As a matter of fact, stray dots may register as answers, so do not let your pencil rest on the answer sheet while you are pondering the correct answer. Also, if your pencil lead breaks or is otherwise defective, ask for another.

Since the answer sheet will be dropped in a slot in the scoring machine, be careful not to bend the corners or get the paper crumpled.

The answer sheet normally has five vertical columns of numbers, with 30 numbers to a column. These numbers correspond to the question numbers in your test booklet. After each number, going across the page are four or five pairs of dotted lines. These short dotted lines have small letters or numbers above them. The first two pairs may also have a "T" or "F" above the letters. This indicates that the first two pairs only are to be used if the questions are of the true-false type. If the questions are multiple choice, disregard the "T" and "F" and pay attention only to the small letters or numbers.

Answer your questions in the manner of the sample that follows:

32. The largest city in the United States is
    A. Washington, D.C.
    B. New York City
    C. Chicago
    D. Detroit
    E. San Francisco

1) Choose the answer you think is best. (New York City is the largest, so "B" is correct.)
2) Find the row of dotted lines numbered the same as the question you are answering. (Find row number 32)
3) Find the pair of dotted lines corresponding to the answer. (Find the pair of lines under the mark "B.")
4) Make a solid black mark between the dotted lines.

VI. BEFORE THE TEST

Common sense will help you find procedures to follow to get ready for an examination. Too many of us, however, overlook these sensible measures. Indeed, nervousness and fatigue have been found to be the most serious reasons why applicants fail to do their best on civil service tests. Here is a list of reminders:

- Begin your preparation early – Don't wait until the last minute to go scurrying around for books and materials or to find out what the position is all about.
- Prepare continuously – An hour a night for a week is better than an all-night cram session. This has been definitely established. What is more, a night a week for a month will return better dividends than crowding your study into a shorter period of time.
- Locate the place of the exam – You have been sent a notice telling you when and where to report for the examination. If the location is in a different town or otherwise unfamiliar to you, it would be well to inquire the best route and learn something about the building.
- Relax the night before the test – Allow your mind to rest. Do not study at all that night. Plan some mild recreation or diversion; then go to bed early and get a good night's sleep.
- Get up early enough to make a leisurely trip to the place for the test – This way unforeseen events, traffic snarls, unfamiliar buildings, etc. will not upset you.
- Dress comfortably – A written test is not a fashion show. You will be known by number and not by name, so wear something comfortable.

- Leave excess paraphernalia at home – Shopping bags and odd bundles will get in your way. You need bring only the items mentioned in the official notice you received; usually everything you need is provided. Do not bring reference books to the exam. They will only confuse those last minutes and be taken away from you when in the test room.
- Arrive somewhat ahead of time – If because of transportation schedules you must get there very early, bring a newspaper or magazine to take your mind off yourself while waiting.
- Locate the examination room – When you have found the proper room, you will be directed to the seat or part of the room where you will sit. Sometimes you are given a sheet of instructions to read while you are waiting. Do not fill out any forms until you are told to do so; just read them and be prepared.
- Relax and prepare to listen to the instructions
- If you have any physical problem that may keep you from doing your best, be sure to tell the test administrator. If you are sick or in poor health, you really cannot do your best on the exam. You can come back and take the test some other time.

VII. AT THE TEST

The day of the test is here and you have the test booklet in your hand. The temptation to get going is very strong. Caution! There is more to success than knowing the right answers. You must know how to identify your papers and understand variations in the type of short-answer question used in this particular examination. Follow these suggestions for maximum results from your efforts:

1) Cooperate with the monitor

The test administrator has a duty to create a situation in which you can be as much at ease as possible. He will give instructions, tell you when to begin, check to see that you are marking your answer sheet correctly, and so on. He is not there to guard you, although he will see that your competitors do not take unfair advantage. He wants to help you do your best.

2) Listen to all instructions

Don't jump the gun! Wait until you understand all directions. In most civil service tests you get more time than you need to answer the questions. So don't be in a hurry. Read each word of instructions until you clearly understand the meaning. Study the examples, listen to all announcements and follow directions. Ask questions if you do not understand what to do.

3) Identify your papers

Civil service exams are usually identified by number only. You will be assigned a number; you must not put your name on your test papers. Be sure to copy your number correctly. Since more than one exam may be given, copy your exact examination title.

4) Plan your time

Unless you are told that a test is a "speed" or "rate of work" test, speed itself is usually not important. Time enough to answer all the questions will be provided, but this does not mean that you have all day. An overall time limit has been set. Divide the total time (in minutes) by the number of questions to determine the approximate time you have for each question.

5) Do not linger over difficult questions

If you come across a difficult question, mark it with a paper clip (useful to have along) and come back to it when you have been through the booklet. One caution if you do this – be sure to skip a number on your answer sheet as well. Check often to be sure that you have not lost your place and that you are marking in the row numbered the same as the question you are answering.

6) Read the questions

Be sure you know what the question asks! Many capable people are unsuccessful because they failed to *read* the questions correctly.

7) Answer all questions

Unless you have been instructed that a penalty will be deducted for incorrect answers, it is better to guess than to omit a question.

8) Speed tests

It is often better NOT to guess on speed tests. It has been found that on timed tests people are tempted to spend the last few seconds before time is called in marking answers at random – without even reading them – in the hope of picking up a few extra points. To discourage this practice, the instructions may warn you that your score will be "corrected" for guessing. That is, a penalty will be applied. The incorrect answers will be deducted from the correct ones, or some other penalty formula will be used.

9) Review your answers

If you finish before time is called, go back to the questions you guessed or omitted to give them further thought. Review other answers if you have time.

10) Return your test materials

If you are ready to leave before others have finished or time is called, take ALL your materials to the monitor and leave quietly. Never take any test material with you. The monitor can discover whose papers are not complete, and taking a test booklet may be grounds for disqualification.

VIII. EXAMINATION TECHNIQUES

1) Read the general instructions carefully. These are usually printed on the first page of the exam booklet. As a rule, these instructions refer to the timing of the examination; the fact that you should not start work until the signal and must stop work at a signal, etc. If there are any *special* instructions, such as a choice of questions to be answered, make sure that you note this instruction carefully.

2) When you are ready to start work on the examination, that is as soon as the signal has been given, read the instructions to each question booklet, underline any key words or phrases, such as *least, best, outline, describe* and the like. In this way you will tend to answer as requested rather than discover on reviewing your paper that you *listed without describing*, that you selected the *worst* choice rather than the *best* choice, etc.

3) If the examination is of the objective or multiple-choice type – that is, each question will also give a series of possible answers: A, B, C or D, and you are called upon to select the best answer and write the letter next to that answer on your answer paper – it is advisable to start answering each question in turn. There may be anywhere from 50 to 100 such questions in the three or four hours allotted and you can see how much time would be taken if you read through all the questions before beginning to answer any. Furthermore, if you come across a question or group of questions which you know would be difficult to answer, it would undoubtedly affect your handling of all the other questions.

4) If the examination is of the essay type and contains but a few questions, it is a moot point as to whether you should read all the questions before starting to answer any one. Of course, if you are given a choice – say five out of seven and the like – then it is essential to read all the questions so you can eliminate the two that are most difficult. If, however, you are asked to answer all the questions, there may be danger in trying to answer the easiest one first because you may find that you will spend too much time on it. The best technique is to answer the first question, then proceed to the second, etc.

5) Time your answers. Before the exam begins, write down the time it started, then add the time allowed for the examination and write down the time it must be completed, then divide the time available somewhat as follows:
    - If 3-1/2 hours are allowed, that would be 210 minutes. If you have 80 objective-type questions, that would be an average of 2-1/2 minutes per question. Allow yourself no more than 2 minutes per question, or a total of 160 minutes, which will permit about 50 minutes to review.
    - If for the time allotment of 210 minutes there are 7 essay questions to answer, that would average about 30 minutes a question. Give yourself only 25 minutes per question so that you have about 35 minutes to review.

6) The most important instruction is to *read each question* and make sure you know what is wanted. The second most important instruction is to *time yourself properly* so that you answer every question. The third most important instruction is to *answer every question*. Guess if you have to but include something for each question. Remember that you will receive no credit for a blank and will probably receive some credit if you write something in answer to an essay question. If you guess a letter – say "B" for a multiple-choice question – you may have guessed right. If you leave a blank as an answer to a multiple-choice question, the examiners may respect your feelings but it will not add a point to your score. Some exams may penalize you for wrong answers, so in such cases *only*, you may not want to guess unless you have some basis for your answer.

7) Suggestions
    a. Objective-type questions
        1. Examine the question booklet for proper sequence of pages and questions
        2. Read all instructions carefully
        3. Skip any question which seems too difficult; return to it after all other questions have been answered
        4. Apportion your time properly; do not spend too much time on any single question or group of questions

5. Note and underline key words – *all, most, fewest, least, best, worst, same, opposite,* etc.
6. Pay particular attention to negatives
7. Note unusual option, e.g., unduly long, short, complex, different or similar in content to the body of the question
8. Observe the use of "hedging" words – *probably, may, most likely,* etc.
9. Make sure that your answer is put next to the same number as the question
10. Do not second-guess unless you have good reason to believe the second answer is definitely more correct
11. Cross out original answer if you decide another answer is more accurate; do not erase until you are ready to hand your paper in
12. Answer all questions; guess unless instructed otherwise
13. Leave time for review

b. Essay questions
1. Read each question carefully
2. Determine exactly what is wanted. Underline key words or phrases.
3. Decide on outline or paragraph answer
4. Include many different points and elements unless asked to develop any one or two points or elements
5. Show impartiality by giving pros and cons unless directed to select one side only
6. Make and write down any assumptions you find necessary to answer the questions
7. Watch your English, grammar, punctuation and choice of words
8. Time your answers; don't crowd material

8) Answering the essay question

Most essay questions can be answered by framing the specific response around several key words or ideas. Here are a few such key words or ideas:

M's: manpower, materials, methods, money, management
P's: purpose, program, policy, plan, procedure, practice, problems, pitfalls, personnel, public relations

a. Six basic steps in handling problems:
1. Preliminary plan and background development
2. Collect information, data and facts
3. Analyze and interpret information, data and facts
4. Analyze and develop solutions as well as make recommendations
5. Prepare report and sell recommendations
6. Install recommendations and follow up effectiveness

b. Pitfalls to avoid
1. *Taking things for granted* – A statement of the situation does not necessarily imply that each of the elements is necessarily true; for example, a complaint may be invalid and biased so that all that can be taken for granted is that a complaint has been registered

2. *Considering only one side of a situation* – Wherever possible, indicate several alternatives and then point out the reasons you selected the best one
3. *Failing to indicate follow up* – Whenever your answer indicates action on your part, make certain that you will take proper follow-up action to see how successful your recommendations, procedures or actions turn out to be
4. *Taking too long in answering any single question* – Remember to time your answers properly

IX. AFTER THE TEST

Scoring procedures differ in detail among civil service jurisdictions although the general principles are the same. Whether the papers are hand-scored or graded by machine we have described, they are nearly always graded by number. That is, the person who marks the paper knows only the number – never the name – of the applicant. Not until all the papers have been graded will they be matched with names. If other tests, such as training and experience or oral interview ratings have been given, scores will be combined. Different parts of the examination usually have different weights. For example, the written test might count 60 percent of the final grade, and a rating of training and experience 40 percent. In many jurisdictions, veterans will have a certain number of points added to their grades.

After the final grade has been determined, the names are placed in grade order and an eligible list is established. There are various methods for resolving ties between those who get the same final grade – probably the most common is to place first the name of the person whose application was received first. Job offers are made from the eligible list in the order the names appear on it. You will be notified of your grade and your rank as soon as all these computations have been made. This will be done as rapidly as possible.

People who are found to meet the requirements in the announcement are called "eligibles." Their names are put on a list of eligible candidates. An eligible's chances of getting a job depend on how high he stands on this list and how fast agencies are filling jobs from the list.

When a job is to be filled from a list of eligibles, the agency asks for the names of people on the list of eligibles for that job. When the civil service commission receives this request, it sends to the agency the names of the three people highest on this list. Or, if the job to be filled has specialized requirements, the office sends the agency the names of the top three persons who meet these requirements from the general list.

The appointing officer makes a choice from among the three people whose names were sent to him. If the selected person accepts the appointment, the names of the others are put back on the list to be considered for future openings.

That is the rule in hiring from all kinds of eligible lists, whether they are for typist, carpenter, chemist, or something else. For every vacancy, the appointing officer has his choice of any one of the top three eligibles on the list. This explains why the person whose name is on top of the list sometimes does not get an appointment when some of the persons lower on the list do. If the appointing officer chooses the second or third eligible, the No. 1 eligible does not get a job at once, but stays on the list until he is appointed or the list is terminated.

X. HOW TO PASS THE INTERVIEW TEST

The examination for which you applied requires an oral interview test. You have already taken the written test and you are now being called for the interview test – the final part of the formal examination.

You may think that it is not possible to prepare for an interview test and that there are no procedures to follow during an interview. Our purpose is to point out some things you can do in advance that will help you and some good rules to follow and pitfalls to avoid while you are being interviewed.

What is an interview supposed to test?

The written examination is designed to test the technical knowledge and competence of the candidate; the oral is designed to evaluate intangible qualities, not readily measured otherwise, and to establish a list showing the relative fitness of each candidate – as measured against his competitors – for the position sought. Scoring is not on the basis of "right" and "wrong," but on a sliding scale of values ranging from "not passable" to "outstanding." As a matter of fact, it is possible to achieve a relatively low score without a single "incorrect" answer because of evident weakness in the qualities being measured.

Occasionally, an examination may consist entirely of an oral test – either an individual or a group oral. In such cases, information is sought concerning the technical knowledges and abilities of the candidate, since there has been no written examination for this purpose. More commonly, however, an oral test is used to supplement a written examination.

Who conducts interviews?

The composition of oral boards varies among different jurisdictions. In nearly all, a representative of the personnel department serves as chairman. One of the members of the board may be a representative of the department in which the candidate would work. In some cases, "outside experts" are used, and, frequently, a businessman or some other representative of the general public is asked to serve. Labor and management or other special groups may be represented. The aim is to secure the services of experts in the appropriate field.

However the board is composed, it is a good idea (and not at all improper or unethical) to ascertain in advance of the interview who the members are and what groups they represent. When you are introduced to them, you will have some idea of their backgrounds and interests, and at least you will not stutter and stammer over their names.

What should be done before the interview?

While knowledge about the board members is useful and takes some of the surprise element out of the interview, there is other preparation which is more substantive. It *is* possible to prepare for an oral interview – in several ways:

1) Keep a copy of your application and review it carefully before the interview

This may be the only document before the oral board, and the starting point of the interview. Know what education and experience you have listed there, and the sequence and dates of all of it. Sometimes the board will ask you to review the highlights of your experience for them; you should not have to hem and haw doing it.

2) Study the class specification and the examination announcement

Usually, the oral board has one or both of these to guide them. The qualities, characteristics or knowledges required by the position sought are stated in these documents. They offer valuable clues as to the nature of the oral interview. For example, if the job involves supervisory responsibilities, the announcement will usually indicate that knowledge of modern supervisory methods and the qualifications of the candidate as a supervisor will be tested. If so, you can expect such questions, frequently in the form of a hypothetical situation which you are expected to solve. NEVER go into an oral without knowledge of the duties and responsibilities of the job you seek.

3) Think through each qualification required

Try to visualize the kind of questions you would ask if you were a board member. How well could you answer them? Try especially to appraise your own knowledge and background in each area, *measured against the job sought*, and identify any areas in which you are weak. Be critical and realistic – do not flatter yourself.

4) Do some general reading in areas in which you feel you may be weak

For example, if the job involves supervision and your past experience has NOT, some general reading in supervisory methods and practices, particularly in the field of human relations, might be useful. Do NOT study agency procedures or detailed manuals. The oral board will be testing your understanding and capacity, not your memory.

5) Get a good night's sleep and watch your general health and mental attitude

You will want a clear head at the interview. Take care of a cold or any other minor ailment, and of course, no hangovers.

What should be done on the day of the interview?

Now comes the day of the interview itself. Give yourself plenty of time to get there. Plan to arrive somewhat ahead of the scheduled time, particularly if your appointment is in the fore part of the day. If a previous candidate fails to appear, the board might be ready for you a bit early. By early afternoon an oral board is almost invariably behind schedule if there are many candidates, and you may have to wait. Take along a book or magazine to read, or your application to review, but leave any extraneous material in the waiting room when you go in for your interview. In any event, relax and compose yourself.

The matter of dress is important. The board is forming impressions about you – from your experience, your manners, your attitude, and your appearance. Give your personal appearance careful attention. Dress your best, but not your flashiest. Choose conservative, appropriate clothing, and be sure it is immaculate. This is a business interview, and your appearance should indicate that you regard it as such. Besides, being well groomed and properly dressed will help boost your confidence.

Sooner or later, someone will call your name and escort you into the interview room. *This is it.* From here on you are on your own. It is too late for any more preparation. But remember, you asked for this opportunity to prove your fitness, and you are here because your request was granted.

What happens when you go in?

The usual sequence of events will be as follows: The clerk (who is often the board stenographer) will introduce you to the chairman of the oral board, who will introduce you to the other members of the board. Acknowledge the introductions before you sit down. Do not be surprised if you find a microphone facing you or a stenotypist sitting by. Oral interviews are usually recorded in the event of an appeal or other review.

Usually the chairman of the board will open the interview by reviewing the highlights of your education and work experience from your application – primarily for the benefit of the other members of the board, as well as to get the material into the record. Do not interrupt or comment unless there is an error or significant misinterpretation; if that is the case, do not hesitate. But do not quibble about insignificant matters. Also, he will usually ask you some question about your education, experience or your present job – partly to get you to start talking and to establish the interviewing "rapport." He may start the actual questioning, or turn it over to one of the other members. Frequently, each member undertakes the questioning on a particular area, one in which he is perhaps most competent, so you can expect each member to participate in the examination. Because time is limited, you may also expect some rather abrupt switches in the direction the questioning takes, so do not be upset by it. Normally, a board member will not pursue a single line of questioning unless he discovers a particular strength or weakness.

After each member has participated, the chairman will usually ask whether any member has any further questions, then will ask you if you have anything you wish to add. Unless you are expecting this question, it may floor you. Worse, it may start you off on an extended, extemporaneous speech. The board is not usually seeking more information. The question is principally to offer you a last opportunity to present further qualifications or to indicate that you have nothing to add. So, if you feel that a significant qualification or characteristic has been overlooked, it is proper to point it out in a sentence or so. Do not compliment the board on the thoroughness of their examination – they have been sketchy, and you know it. If you wish, merely say, "No thank you, I have nothing further to add." This is a point where you can "talk yourself out" of a good impression or fail to present an important bit of information. Remember, *you close the interview yourself.*

The chairman will then say, "That is all, Mr. _____, thank you." Do not be startled; the interview is over, and quicker than you think. Thank him, gather your belongings and take your leave. Save your sigh of relief for the other side of the door.

How to put your best foot forward

Throughout this entire process, you may feel that the board individually and collectively is trying to pierce your defenses, seek out your hidden weaknesses and embarrass and confuse you. Actually, this is not true. They are obliged to make an appraisal of your qualifications for the job you are seeking, and they want to see you in your best light. Remember, they must interview all candidates and a non-cooperative candidate may become a failure in spite of their best efforts to bring out his qualifications. Here are 15 suggestions that will help you:

1) Be natural – Keep your attitude confident, not cocky

If you are not confident that you can do the job, do not expect the board to be. Do not apologize for your weaknesses, try to bring out your strong points. The board is interested in a positive, not negative, presentation. Cockiness will antagonize any board member and make him wonder if you are covering up a weakness by a false show of strength.

2) Get comfortable, but don't lounge or sprawl

Sit erectly but not stiffly. A careless posture may lead the board to conclude that you are careless in other things, or at least that you are not impressed by the importance of the occasion. Either conclusion is natural, even if incorrect. Do not fuss with your clothing, a pencil or an ashtray. Your hands may occasionally be useful to emphasize a point; do not let them become a point of distraction.

3) Do not wisecrack or make small talk

This is a serious situation, and your attitude should show that you consider it as such. Further, the time of the board is limited – they do not want to waste it, and neither should you.

4) Do not exaggerate your experience or abilities

In the first place, from information in the application or other interviews and sources, the board may know more about you than you think. Secondly, you probably will not get away with it. An experienced board is rather adept at spotting such a situation, so do not take the chance.

5) If you know a board member, do not make a point of it, yet do not hide it

Certainly you are not fooling him, and probably not the other members of the board. Do not try to take advantage of your acquaintanceship – it will probably do you little good.

6) Do not dominate the interview

Let the board do that. They will give you the clues – do not assume that you have to do all the talking. Realize that the board has a number of questions to ask you, and do not try to take up all the interview time by showing off your extensive knowledge of the answer to the first one.

7) Be attentive

You only have 20 minutes or so, and you should keep your attention at its sharpest throughout. When a member is addressing a problem or question to you, give him your undivided attention. Address your reply principally to him, but do not exclude the other board members.

8) Do not interrupt

A board member may be stating a problem for you to analyze. He will ask you a question when the time comes. Let him state the problem, and wait for the question.

9) Make sure you understand the question

Do not try to answer until you are sure what the question is. If it is not clear, restate it in your own words or ask the board member to clarify it for you. However, do not haggle about minor elements.

10) Reply promptly but not hastily

A common entry on oral board rating sheets is "candidate responded readily," or "candidate hesitated in replies." Respond as promptly and quickly as you can, but do not jump to a hasty, ill-considered answer.

11) Do not be peremptory in your answers

A brief answer is proper – but do not fire your answer back. That is a losing game from your point of view. The board member can probably ask questions much faster than you can answer them.

12) Do not try to create the answer you think the board member wants

He is interested in what kind of mind you have and how it works – not in playing games. Furthermore, he can usually spot this practice and will actually grade you down on it.

13) Do not switch sides in your reply merely to agree with a board member

Frequently, a member will take a contrary position merely to draw you out and to see if you are willing and able to defend your point of view. Do not start a debate, yet do not surrender a good position. If a position is worth taking, it is worth defending.

14) Do not be afraid to admit an error in judgment if you are shown to be wrong

The board knows that you are forced to reply without any opportunity for careful consideration. Your answer may be demonstrably wrong. If so, admit it and get on with the interview.

15) Do not dwell at length on your present job

The opening question may relate to your present assignment. Answer the question but do not go into an extended discussion. You are being examined for a *new* job, not your present one. As a matter of fact, try to phrase ALL your answers in terms of the job for which you are being examined.

Basis of Rating

Probably you will forget most of these "do's" and "don'ts" when you walk into the oral interview room. Even remembering them all will not ensure you a passing grade. Perhaps you did not have the qualifications in the first place. But remembering them will help you to put your best foot forward, without treading on the toes of the board members.

Rumor and popular opinion to the contrary notwithstanding, an oral board wants you to make the best appearance possible. They know you are under pressure – but they also want to see how you respond to it as a guide to what your reaction would be under the pressures of the job you seek. They will be influenced by the degree of poise you display, the personal traits you show and the manner in which you respond.

ABOUT THIS BOOK

This book contains tests divided into Examination Sections. Go through each test, answering every question in the margin. We have also attached a sample answer sheet at the back of the book that can be removed and used. At the end of each test look at the answer key and check your answers. On the ones you got wrong, look at the right answer choice and learn. Do not fill in the answers first. Do not memorize the questions and answers, but understand the answer and principles involved. On your test, the questions will likely be different from the samples. Questions are changed and new ones added. If you understand these past questions you should have success with any changes that arise. Tests may consist of several types of questions. We have additional books on each subject should more study be advisable or necessary for you. Finally, the more you study, the better prepared you will be. This book is intended to be the last thing you study before you walk into the examination room. Prior study of relevant texts is also recommended. NLC publishes some of these in our Fundamental Series. Knowledge and good sense are important factors in passing your exam. Good luck also helps. So now study this Passbook, absorb the material contained within and take that knowledge into the examination. Then do your best to pass that exam.

EXAMINATION SECTION

EXAMINATION SECTION
TEST 1

DIRECTIONS: Each question or incomplete statement is followed by several suggested answers or completions. Select the one that BEST answers the question or completes the statement. *PRINT THE LETTER OF THE CORRECT ANSWER IN THE SPACE AT THE RIGHT.*

1. The flow of oil in an automatic rotary cup oil burner is regulated by a(n)

    A. thermostat
    B. metering valve
    C. pressure relief valve
    D. electric eye

2. The type of fuel which must be *pre-heated* before it can be burned efficiently is

    A. natural gas
    B. pea coal
    C. Number 2 oil
    D. Number 6 oil

3. A suction gauge in a fuel-oil transfer system is *usually* located

    A. *before* the strainer
    B. *after* the strainer and *before* the pump
    C. *after* the pump and *before* the pressure relief valve
    D. *after* the pressure relief valve

4. The FIRST item that should be checked before starting the fire in a steam boiler is the

    A. thermostat
    B. vacuum pump
    C. boiler water level
    D. steam pressure

5. Operation of a boiler that has been *sealed* by the department of buildings is

    A. prohibited
    B. permitted when the outside temperature is below 32° F
    C. permitted between the hours of 6:00 A.M. and 8:00 A.M. and 9:00 P.M. and 11:00 P.M.
    D. permitted only for the purposes of heating domestic water

6. Lowering the thermostat setting by 5 degrees during the heating season will result in a fuel saving of, *most nearly,* _____ percent.

    A. 2 B. 5 C. 20 D. 50

7. An electrically-driven rotary fuel oil pump must be protected from internal damage by the installation in the oil line of a

    A. discharge-side strainer
    B. check valve
    C. suction gauge
    D. pressure relief valve

8. The air pollution code states that no person shall cause or permit the emission of an air contaminant of a density which appears as dark or darker than Number _____ on the standard smoke chart.

    A. One
    B. Two
    C. Three
    D. Four

9. When a glass globe is put back over a newly-replaced light bulb in a ceiling light fixture, the holding screws on the globe should be tightened, then loosened one half turn.
   This is done MAINLY to prevent

   A. fires caused by electrical short circuits
   B. cracking of the globe due to heat expansion
   C. falling of the globe from the light fixture
   D. building up of harmful gases inside the globe

10. Standard 120-volt plug-type fuses are *generally* rated in

   A. farads   B. ohms   C. watts   D. amperes

11. Standard 120-volt electric light bulbs are *generally* rated in

   A. farads   B. ohms   C. watts   D. amperes

12. A cleaner informs you that his electrical vacuum cleaner is not working even though he tried the off-on switch several times and checked to see that the plug was still in the wall outlet.
    Of the following, the FIRST course of action you should take in this situation is to

    A. determine if the circuit-breaker has tripped out
    B. take apart the vacuum cleaner
    C. replace the electric cord on the vacuum cleaner
    D. replace the electrical outlet

13. The one of the following that is the MOST practical method for a building custodian to use in making a temporary repair in a straight portion of a water pipe which has a small leak is to

    A. attach a clamped patch over the leak
    B. weld or braze the pipe, depending on the material
    C. drill and tap the pipe, then insert a plug
    D. fill the hole with an epoxy sealer

14. The PRIMARY function of the packing which is generally found in the stuffing box of a centrifugal pump is to

    A. compensate for misalignment of the pump shaft
    B. prevent leakage of the fluid
    C. control the discharge rate of the pump
    D. provide support for the pump shaft

15. A pipe coupling is a plumbing fitting that is *most commonly* used to join

    A. two pieces of threaded pipe of the same diameter
    B. a large diameter tubing to a smaller diameter threaded pipe
    C. two pieces of threaded pipe of different diameters
    D. a large diameter threaded pipe to a smaller diameter tubing

16. Of the following, the MOST important reason for replacing a worn washer in a dripping faucet as soon as possible is to prevent   16.____

   A. overflow of the sink tap
   B. the mixture of hot and cold water in the sink
   C. damage to the faucet parts that can be the result of overtightening the stem
   D. air from entering the supply line

17. Window glass is secured mechanically in wood windows by   17.____

   A. glazing points   B. enamel paint
   C. screws   D. putty

18. In carpentry work, the *most commonly* used hand saw is the _____ saw.   18.____

   A. hack   B. rip   C. buck   D. cross-cut

19. The device which *usually* keeps a doorknob from rotating on the spindle is a   19.____

   A. cotter pin   B. tapered key
   C. set screw   D. stop screw

20. The *one* of the following types of nails that *usually* requires the use of a tool known as a nail set is the _____ nail.   20.____

   A. finishing   B. sheet rock   C. 6-penny   D. cut

21. The following tasks are frequently done when an office is cleaned: 21.____
      I. The floor is vacuumed.
      II. The ash trays and waste baskets are emptied.
      III. The desks and furniture are dusted.
   The ORDER in which these tasks should *generally* be done is:

   A. I, II, III   B. II, III, I   C. III, II, I   D. I, III, II

22. When wax is applied to a floor by the use of a twine mop with handle, the wax should be _____ with the mop.   22.____

   A. applied in thin coats
   B. applied in heavy coats
   C. poured on the floor, then spread
   D. dropped on the floor, then spread

23. The BEST way to clean dust from an accoustical-type ceiling is with a   23.____

   A. strong soap solution   B. wet sponge
   C. vacuum cleaner   D. stream of water

24. Of the following, the MOST important reason why a wet mop should NOT be wrung out by hand is that   24.____

   A. the strings of the mop will be damaged by hand-wringing
   B. sharp objects picked up by the mop may injure the hands
   C. the mop cannot be made dry enough by hand-wringing
   D. fine dirt will become embedded in the strings of the mop

25. When a painted wall is washed by hand, the wall should be washed from the

   A. *top down,* with a soaking *wet* sponge
   B. *bottom up,* with a soaking *wet* sponge
   C. *top down,* with a *damp* sponge
   D. *bottom up,* with a *damp* sponge

26. When a painted wall is brushed with a clean lamb's wool duster, the duster should be drawn _____ with a _____ pressure.

   A. *downward; light*
   B. *upward; light*
   C. *downward; firm*
   D. *upward; firm*

27. The *one* of the following terms which BEST describes the size of a floor brush is

   A. 72-cubic inch
   B. 32-ounce
   C. 24-inch
   D. 10-square foot

28. Terrazzo floors should be mopped periodically with a(n)

   A. acid solution
   B. neutral detergent in warm water
   C. mop treated with kerosene
   D. strong alkaline solution

29. The MAIN reason why the handle of a reversible floor brush should be shifted from one side of the brush block to the opposite side is to

   A. change the angle at which the brush sweeps the floor
   B. give equal wear to both sides of the brush
   C. permit the brush to sweep hard-to-reach areas
   D. make it easier to sweep backward

30. When a long corridor is swept with a floor brush, it is *good* practice to

   A. push the brush with moderately long strokes and flick it after each stroke
   B. press on the brush and push it the whole length of the corridor in one sweep
   C. pull the brush inward with short, brisk strokes
   D. sweep across rather than down the length of the corridor

KEY (CORRECT ANSWERS)

1.	B	16.	C
2.	D	17.	A
3.	B	18.	D
4.	C	19.	C
5.	A	20.	A
6.	C	21.	B
7.	D	22.	A
8.	B	23.	C
9.	B	24.	B
10.	D	25.	D
11.	C	26.	A
12.	A	27.	C
13.	A	28.	B
14.	B	29.	B
15.	A	30.	A

TEST 2

DIRECTIONS: Each question or incomplete statement is followed by several suggested answers or completions. Select the one that BEST answers the question or completes the statement. *PRINT THE LETTER OF THE CORRECT ANSWER IN THE SPACE AT THE RIGHT.*

1. Of the following office cleaning jobs performed during the year, the *one* which should be done MOST frequently is

   A. cleaning the fluorescent lights
   B. dusting the Venetian blinds
   C. cleaning the bookcase glass
   D. carpet-sweeping the rug

   1.___

2. The BEST polishing agent to use on wood furniture is

   A. pumice   B. paste wax
   C. water emulsion wax   D. neat's-foot oil

   2.___

3. Lemon oil polish is used BEST to polish

   A. exterior bronze   B. marble walls
   C. leather seats   D. lacquered metal

   3.___

4. Cleaning with trisodium phosphate is *most likely* to damage

   A. toilet bowls   B. drain pipes
   C. polished marble floors D. rubber tile floors

   4.___

5. Of the following cleaning agents, the one which should NOT be used to remove stains from urinals is

   A. caustic lye   B. detergent
   C. oxalic acid   D. muriatic acid

   5.___

6. The one of the following cleaners which *generally* contains an abrasive is

   A. caustic lye   B. trisodium phosphate
   C. scouring powder   D. ammonia

   6.___

7. The instructions on a box of cleaning powder say: *Mix one pound of cleaning powder in four gallons of water.* According to these instructions, how many ounces of cleaning powder should be mixed in one gallon of water?

   A. 4   B. 8   C. 12   D. 16

   7.___

8. In accordance with recommended practice, a dust mop, when not being used, should be stored

   A. *hanging*, handle end down
   B. *hanging*, handle end up
   C. *standing* on the floor, handle end down
   D. *standing* on the floor, handle end up

   8.___

9. The two types of floors found in public buildings are classified as *hard floors* and *soft floors*.
An example of a *hard floor* is one made of

   A. linoleum
   B. cork
   C. ceramic tile
   D. asphalt tile

10. A squeegee is a tool that is MAINLY used to clean

    A. painted walls
    B. radiator covers
    C. window glass
    D. ceramic tile floors

11. The BEST way for a building custodian to determine whether a cleaner is doing his work well is by

    A. observing the cleaner at work for several hours
    B. asking the cleaner questions about the work
    C. asking other cleaners to rate his work
    D. inspecting the cleanliness of the spaces assigned to the cleaner

12. The PRIMARY purpose of using a disinfectant material is to

    A. kill germs
    B. destroy odors
    C. remove stains
    D. kill insects

13. Windows should be washed by using a solution of warm water mixed with

    A. chlorine bleach
    B. kerosene
    C. ammonia
    D. soft soap

14. Of the following, the MOST effective way to reduce waste of cleaning tools is to

    A. keep careful records of how often tools are issued
    B. require that the old tool be returned before issuing a new one
    C. require that all tools be used for a fixed number of hours before replacing them
    D. train the cleaners to use the tools properly

15. The number of square feet of unobstructed corridor floor space that a cleaner should sweep in an hour is, *most nearly*,

    A. 1200   B. 2400   C. 4000   D. 6000

16. Sweeping compound is used on concrete floors MAINLY to

    A. polish the floor
    B. keep the dust down
    C. soften the encrusted dirt
    D. provide a non-slip surface

17. The BEST attachment to use on an electric scrubbing machine when stripping waxed resilient flooring is a

    A. nylon disk
    B. soft brush
    C. steel wool pad
    D. pumice wheel

18. A counter brush is BEST suited to cleaning

    A. water cooler drains
    B. radiators
    C. light fixtures
    D. lavatory fixtures

19. Improper use of a carbon-dioxide type portable fire extinguisher may cause injury to the operator because

    A. handling the nozzle during discharge can cause frostbite to the skin
    B. carbon dioxide is highly poisonous if breathed into the lungs
    C. use of carbon dioxide on an oil fire can cause a chemical explosion
    D. the powdery residue left by the discharge is highly caustic to the skin

20. When using a portable single ladder with ten rungs, the GREATEST number of rungs that a cleaner should climb up is

    A. 7   B. 8   C. 9   D. 10

21. Of the following types of portable fire extinguishers, the one which should be used to control a fire in or around live electrical equipment is the _____ type.

    A. foam
    B. soda-acid
    C. carbon-dioxide
    D. gas-cartridge water

22. The MOST frequent cause of accidental injuries to workers on the job is

    A. unsafe working practices of employees
    B. poor design of buildings and working areas
    C. lack of warning signs in hazardous working areas
    D. lack of adequate safety guards on equipment and machinery

23. Of the following, the MOST important purpose of preparing an accident report on an injury to a cleaner is to help

    A. collect statistics on different types of accidents
    B. calm the feelings of the injured cleaner
    C. prevent similar accidents in the future
    D. prove that the cleaner was at fault

24. The one of the following types of locks that is used on emergency exit doors is the _____ bolt.

    A. panic   B. dead   C. cinch   D. toggle

25. The one of the following types of locks that *usually* contains both a live bolt and a dead bolt is a _____ lock.

    A. mortise
    B. double-hung window
    C. loose pin butt
    D. window frame

KEY (CORRECT ANSWERS)

1. D
2. B
3. A
4. C
5. D

6. C
7. A
8. B
9. C
10. C

11. D
12. A
13. C
14. D
15. D

16. B
17. A
18. B
19. A
20. B

21. C
22. A
23. C
24. A
25. A

EXAMINATION SECTION
TEST 1

DIRECTIONS: Each question or incomplete statement is followed by several suggested answers or completions. Select the one that BEST answers the question or completes the statement. *PRINT THE LETTER OF THE CORRECT ANSWER IN THE SPACE AT THE RIGHT.*

1. A chemical frequently used to melt ice on outdoor pavements is   1.____

    A. ammonia
    B. soda
    C. carbon tetrachloride
    D. calcium chloride

2. A herbicide is a chemical PRIMARILY used as a(n)   2.____

    A. disinfectant
    B. fertilizer
    C. insect killer
    D. weed killer

3. Established plants that continue to blossom year after year without reseeding are GENERALLY known as   3.____

    A. annuals
    B. parasites
    C. perennials
    D. symbiotics

4. A ferrous sulfate solution is sometimes used to treat shrubs or trees that have a deficiency of   4.____

    A. boron   B. copper   C. iron   D. zinc

5. A tree is described as *deciduous*.
    This means that it   5.____

    A. bears nuts instead of fruit
    B. has been pruned recently
    C. usually grows in swampy ground
    D. loses its leaves in fall

6. The landscape drawings for a school indicate the planting of *Acer platanoides* at a certain location on the grounds. Acer platanoides is a type of   6.____

    A. privet hedge
    B. rose bush
    C. maple tree
    D. tulip bed

7. After a snowfall has stopped, the law requires that all snow be removed from sidewalks within _____ hour(s).   7.____

    A. 4   B. 3   C. 2   D. 1

8. When roofing material is specified as 5 *ply, 70 lbs.*, it means that, as laid, the total of 5 plies weighs 70 lbs. per 100   8.____

    A. square feet
    B. yards length
    C. square inches
    D. feet length

9. Little white insects that look like small shrimps and feed on the roots of grass are called

    A. grubs
    B. ticks
    C. praying mantes
    D. crabs

10. A term used to indicate a lawn chemical weed killer is

    A. germicide
    B. emulsified
    C. herbicide
    D. vitrified

11. Before starting any lawn mowing, the distance between the blade and a flat surface should be measured with a ruler. This distance should be such that the cut of the grass above the ground is _____ inch(es).

    A. 1 B. 1½ C. 2 D. 3

12. *Neat* cement is a mixture of cement

    A. putty and water
    B. and water
    C. lime and water
    D. salt and water

13. In a concrete mix of 1:2:4, the 2 refers to the amount of

    A. sand B. cement C. stone D. water

14. If it is not possible to plant new shrubs immediately upon delivery in the spring, they should be stored in a(n)

    A. sheltered outdoor area
    B. unsheltered outdoor area
    C. boiler room
    D. warm place indoors

15. To remove chalk marks on sidewalks and cemented playground areas, the MOST acceptable cleaning method is

    A. using a brush with warm water
    B. using a brush with warm water containing some kerosene
    C. hosing down such areas with water
    D. using a brush with a solution of muriatic acid in water

16. The *10* in a 10-6-4 mixture stands for the amount of

    A. phoric acid
    B. oxygen
    C. potash
    D. nitrogen

17. Turning over of a lawn is BEST performed during the

    A. spring B. summer C. fall D. winter

18. When watering lawns, an open top can should be placed near the sprinkler and watering should be stopped when the can is filled to a depth of _____ inch(es).

    A. ½ B. 1 C. 1½ D. 2

19. Powered lawnmowers should be filled with gas ONLY

    A. in the boiler room
    B. in the outside storeroom
    C. outdoors
    D. when running

Questions 20-22.

DIRECTIONS: Questions 20 through 22 are to be answered on the basis of the following paragraph.

Whether a main lobby or upper corridor requires scrubbing or mopping and whether it should be done nightly or less frequently depends on the nature of the floor surface and the amount of traffic. In a building with heavy traffic, it may be desirable every night to scrub the main lobby and to mop the upper floors. In such cases, it may also be found desirable to scrub the upper floors once a week. If traffic is light, it may only be necessary to mop the main lobby every other night and to mop the upper floor corridors once a week. If there is any traffic or usage at all, it will be necessary to at least sweep the corridors nightly.

20. According to the above paragraph, in a building with light traffic, the upper floors and corridors should be

    A. swept every other night
    B. mopped every night
    C. swept nightly
    D. mopped every other night

21. The number of times a floor is cleaned depends

    A. mainly on the type of floor surface
    B. mainly on the type of traffic
    C. only on the amount of traffic
    D. on both the floor surface and the amount of traffic

22. It may be desirable to have a heavily used main lobby swept

    A. daily and scrubbed weekly
    B. daily and mopped weekly
    C. and mopped weekly
    D. and scrubbed daily

23. Interior fire alarm systems are tested

    A. daily   B. weekly
    C. every Saturday   D. never

24. An electrical meter is read from

    A. left to right   B. right to left
    C. closest high number D. closest low number

25. A light bulb socket has the threaded shell connected to _____ wire(s).

    A. neither hot nor ground   B. ground
    C. hot   D. hot and ground

KEY (CORRECT ANSWERS)

1.	D	11.	C
2.	D	12.	B
3.	C	13.	A
4.	C	14.	A
5.	D	15.	A
6.	C	16.	D
7.	A	17.	C
8.	A	18.	B
9.	A	19.	C
10.	C	20.	C

21. D
22. D
23. A
24. A
25. B

TEST 2

DIRECTIONS: Each question or incomplete statement is followed by several suggested answers or completions. Select the one that BEST answers the question or completes the statement. *PRINT THE LETTER OF THE CORRECT ANSWER IN THE SPACE AT THE RIGHT.*

1. The purpose of an air valve in a heating system is to   1.____

   A. prevent pressure build-up in a room
   B. relieve air from radiators
   C. allow excess steam to escape from boiler
   D. control room temperature

2. A scale pocket is MOST often found on the   2.____

   A. bottom of steam riser
   B. hot air exhaust grills
   C. hot water radiator
   D. inside of the steam radiator

3. Ventilation of rooms without windows is accomplished by   3.____

   A. opening and closing room doors
   B. heating and cooling of room by radiators
   C. mechanical circulation and exhausting through ducts
   D. use of air deodorizers

4. When a radiator in a one-pipe gravity system is air-bound, the MOST likely cause is   4.____

   A. a defective air valve
   B. air entering through leaking valve
   C. insufficient steam pressure
   D. a defective gate valve

5. When a radiator in a two-pipe gravity system is air-bound, the MOST likely cause is   5.____

   A. a defective air valve
   B. air entering through leaking valve
   C. insufficient steam pressure
   D. a defective gate valve

6. A vacuum heating system does NOT have   6.____

   A. traps
   B. pneumatic valves
   C. risers
   D. air valves

7. In a one-pipe gravity return system,   7.____

   A. piping is large
   B. piping is small
   C. valves can be throttled
   D. vacuum pumps are used

8. One of the advantages of a vacuum system of heating is   8.____

   A. high maintenance costs
   B. use of electricity
   C. low pressure steam circulation
   D. cannot install radiation below the water line

9. A plenum chamber is where

   A. fresh air is filtered
   B. fresh air is heated
   C. returns are heated
   D. steam is reheated

10. Air picks up heat and moisture when compressed. Because of this, compressed air storage tanks should be drained

    A. daily
    B. when gauge glass is full
    C. monthly
    D. weekly

11. The _____ safety devices will shut down an oil burner in the event of flame failure.

    A. fireye
    B. flame rod
    C. stack switch
    D. all of the above

12. Steam is used to heat fuel oil.
    After it has condensed to water, it is

    A. blown down to waste
    B. returned to boiler
    C. used for heating coils
    D. recirculated

13. Relief valves throughout oil flow systems guard the system against excess

    A. temperature
    B. vacuum
    C. pressure
    D. all of the above

14. A transformer is used to raise line voltage for an ignition system.
    This type of voltage increase can be called a(n)

    A. rheostat
    B. amplifying circuit
    C. compensating motor
    D. electrode

15. A device which basically causes hi and low fire conditions in an oil burner is called a

    A. modutrol motor
    B. hi-limit pressuretrol
    C. primary air fan casing
    D. metering valve

16. A device that mixes the proper amount of oil, primary air, and secondary air for combustion is called a

    A. modutrol motor
    B. hi-limit pressuretrol
    C. primary air fan casing
    D. metering valve

17. A device which stops an oil burner in the event of pressuretrol failure is called a

    A. modutrol motor
    B. hi-limit pressuretrol
    C. primary air fan casing
    D. metering valve

18. If the heart of an oil flow system and oil burner operation is the fuel oil transfer pump, the *brain* of this system could be called the

    A. stack switch
    B. aquastat
    C. ringelmann
    D. programmer

19. The spinning cup of the oil burner should be cleaned daily. If oil deposits have hardened on the spinning cup, you should clean it with

    A. a smooth wood or plastic stick
    B. a file
    C. sandpaper
    D. 00 steel wool

20. The BEST method of connecting two No. 14 electrical fixture wires together is with   20.____

    A. solder
    B. screw and nut
    C. tape
    D. twist wires together

21. A safety device used instead of a fuse to protect electrical equipment against overload is a   21.____

    A. rheostat
    B. circuit breaker
    C. relay
    D. toggle switch

22. Piping used to carry exposed electrical wiring is called   22.____

    A. conductors
    B. sleeves
    C. conduit
    D. leaders

23. Knife switches may be made to work more easily by using   23.____

    A. vaseline   B. graphite   C. soapstone   D. grease

24. Hidden electrical wiring is carried in   24.____

    A. conduit   B. raceway   C. conductors   D. BX cable

25. A T-40 could be BEST described as a(n)   25.____

    A. fuse
    B. incandescent lamp
    C. fluorescent bulb
    D. circuit breaker

KEY (CORRECT ANSWERS)

1.	B	11.	D
2.	A	12.	A
3.	C	13.	C
4.	A	14.	B
5.	A	15.	D
6.	D	16.	A
7.	A	17.	B
8.	C	18.	D
9.	B	19.	A
10.	D	20.	A

21. B
22. C
23. C
24. D
25. B

EXAMINATION SECTION
TEST 1

DIRECTIONS: Each question or incomplete statement is followed by several suggested answers or completions. Select the one that BEST answers the question or completes the statement. *PRINT THE LETTER OF THE CORRECT ANSWER IN THE SPACE AT THE RIGHT.*

1. In the wintertime, the FIRST thing a custodian does in the morning, after throwing the main switch, is to
    A. take a reading of the electric meter
    B. prepare his daily report of fuel consumption
    C. prepare sweeping compound
    D. inspect the water gauge of his boilers

    1.____

2. Rubbish, stones, sticks, and papers on lawns in front of school buildings are MOST effectively collected by means of a
    A. 30 inch floor brush with thickly set bristles
    B. corn broom
    C. 4 foot pole with a nail set in the bottom of it
    D. rake

    2.____

3. Which of the following statements about sweeping is NOT correct?
    A. Corridors and stairs should not be swept during school hours.
    B. Classrooms should usually be swept daily after the close of the afternoon session.
    C. Dry sweeping is not to be used in classrooms or corridors.
    D. Special rooms, as sewing rooms, may be swept during school hours if unoccupied.

    3.____

4. The PROPER size of floor brush to be used in classrooms with fixed seats is _____ inches.
    A. 36   B. 24   C. 16   D. 6

    4.____

5. Sweeping compound made of oiled sawdust should NOT be used on _____ floors.
    A. cement   B. rubber tile
    C. oiled wood   D. composition

    5.____

6. In oiling a wood floor, it is GOOD practice to
    A. apply the oil with a dipped mop up to the baseboards of the walls
    B. avoid application of oil closer than 6 inches of the baseboards
    C. keep the oil about one inch from the baseboard
    D. make sure that oil is applied to the floors under radiators

    6.____

7. Of the following, the LEAST desirable agent for cleaning blackboards is 7.____
   A. damp cloth
   B. clear warm water applied with a sponge
   C. warm water with a little kerosene
   D. warm water containing a mild soap solution

8. Chalk trays of blackboards should be washed and cleaned 8.____
   A. once a week
   B. daily
   C. only when the teacher reports cleaning needed
   D. once a month

9. In cleaning rooms by means of a central vacuum cleaning system, 9.____
   A. sweeping compound is used merely to prevent dust from rising
   B. rooms need cleaning only twice a week because the machine takes up the oil
   C. wood floors must be oiled more frequently as the machine takes up the oil
   D. the cleaner should not press down upon the tool but should guide it across the floor

10. A gas leak is suspected in the home economics class of a school. 10.____
    The procedure in locating the leak is to
    A. use a lighted match
    B. use a safety lamp
    C. place nose close to line and smell each section
    D. use soapsuds

11. The MOST important reason for placing asbestos jackets on steam lines is to 11.____
    A. prevent persons from burning their hands
    B. prevent heat loss
    C. protect the lines from injury
    D. make the lines appear more presentable

12. If the flag is used on a speaker's platform, it should be displayed 12.____
    A. above and behind the speaker
    B. as a drape over the front of the platform
    C. as a rosette over the speaker's head
    D. as a cover over the speaker's desk

13. When the flag of the United States of America is displayed from a staff 13.____
    projecting from the front of the building, it should be
    A. extended to the tip of the staff
    B. extended to about one foot from the tip of the staff
    C. secured so that there is a sag in the line
    D. extended slowly to the tip of the staff and then drawn back rapidly about 15 inches

14. The common soda-acid fire extinguisher should be checked and refilled
    A. every week
    B. every month
    C. once a year
    D. only if used

15. A small fire has broken out in an electric motor in a sump pump. The lubricant has apparently caught fire.
    The PROPER extinguisher to use is
    A. sand
    B. carbon tetrachloride (pyrene) fire extinguisher
    C. soda-acid fire extinguisher
    D. water under pressure from a hose

16. While cleaning windows, an employee falls from the fourth floor of the building to the sidewalk. The custodian finds the man unconscious.
    The custodian should
    A. move the man into a more comfortable position near the wall of the building and then call a doctor
    B. try to revive the man by depressing his head slightly and applying artificial respiration
    C. hail a taxi and bring the man to a hospital for treatment
    D. phone for an ambulance and cover the man to keep him warm

17. The duties of a custodian include the knowledge of safety rules to prevent accidents and injuries to his employees and himself.
    Of the following, the LEAST harmful practice is to
    A. carry a scraper in the pocket with the blade down
    B. measure the cleaning powder with your hands before placing the powder in water
    C. wet the hands before using steel wool
    D. use lye to clean paint brushes

18. The MOST important reason for not wringing out a mop by hand is that
    A. water cannot be removed effectively in this way
    B. it is not fair to the cleaner
    C. the dirt remains on the mop after the water is removed
    D. pins, nail, or other sharp objects may be picked up and cut the hand, causing an infection

19. The method of using a ladder which you would consider LEAST safe is:
    A. Grasping the side rails of the ladder instead of the rungs when going up
    B. To see that the door is secured wide open when working on a ladder at a door
    C. Leaning weight toward ladder while working on it
    D. Standing on top of the ladder to reach working place

20. When a window pane is broken, the FIRST step the custodian takes is to
    A. remove broken glass from floors and window sill
    B. determine the cause

C. remove the putty with a putty knife
D. prepare a piece of glass to replace the broken pane

21. Your instructions to a cleaner about the proper sweeping of offices should include the following instruction:
    A. Do not move chairs and wastebaskets from their places when sweeping
    B. Place chairs and baskets on the desks to get them out of the way
    C. Set aside the loose small furniture and chairs in an orderly manner when sweeping office floors
    D. Move the desks and chair to the side of the room close to the wall in order to sweep properly

21._____

22. To remove dirt accumulations after the completion of the sweeping task, brushes should be
    A. tapped on the floor in the normal sweeping position
    B. struck on the floor against the side of the block
    C. struck on the floor against the end of the block
    D. turned upside down and the handle tapped on the floor

22._____

23. To sweep rough cement floors in a basement, the BEST tool to use is a
    A. deck brush   B. new 30" floor brush
    C. corn broom   D. treated mop

23._____

24. When a floor is scrubbed, it is NOT correct to
    A. use a steady, even rotary motion
    B. rinse the floor with clean hot water
    C. have the mop strokes follow the boards when drying the floor
    D. wet the floor first by pouring several bucketsful of water on it

24._____

25. Flushing with a hose is MOST appropriate as a method of cleaning
    A. terrazzo floors of corridors
    B. untreated wood floors
    C. linoleum floor where not in frequent use
    D. cement floors

25._____

KEY (CORRECT ANSWERS)

1.	D	11.	B
2.	D	12.	A
3.	A	13.	A
4.	C	14.	C
5.	B	15.	B
6.	D	16.	D
7.	C	17.	A
8.	A	18.	D
9.	D	19.	D
10.	D	20.	A

21.	C
22.	A
23.	C
24.	D
25.	D

TEST 2

DIRECTIONS: Each question or incomplete statement is followed by several suggested answers or completions. Select the one that BEST answers the question or completes the statement. *PRINT THE LETTER OF THE CORRECT ANSWER IN THE SPACE AT THE RIGHT.*

Questions 1-5.

DIRECTIONS: Column I lists cleaning jobs. Column II lists cleansing agents and devices. Select the proper cleansing agent from Column II for each job in Column I. Place the letter of the cleansing agent selected in the space at the right corresponding to the number of the cleansing job.

COLUMN I	COLUMN II	
1. Chewing gum	A. Muriatic acid	1.___
2. Ink stains	B. Broad bladed knife	2.___
3. Fingermarks on glass	C. Kerosene	3.___
4. Rust stains on porcelain	D. Oxalic acid	4.___
5. Hardened dirt on porcelain	E. Lye	5.___
	F. Linseed oil	

6. When the bristles of a floor brush have worn short, the brush should be   6.___
   A. thrown away and the handles saved
   B. saved and the brush used on rough cement floors
   C. saved and used for high dusting in classrooms
   D. saved and used for the weekly scrubbing of linoleum floors

7. Feather dusters should NOT be used because they   7.___
   A. take more time to use than other dusters
   B. cannot be cleaned
   C. do not take up the dust but merely move it from one place to another
   D. do not stir up the dust and streak the furniture with dust rails

8. Floors that are usually NOT waxed are those made of   8.___
   A. pine wood   B. mastic tile   C. rubber tile   D. terrazzo

9. For sweeping under radiators and other inaccessible places, the MOST appropriate tool is the   9.___
   A. counter brush   B. dry mop
   C. feather duster   D. 16" floor brush

10. A cleansing agent that should NOT be used in the cleaning of windows is
    A. water containing fine pumice
    B. water containing a small amount of ammonia
    C. water containing a little kerosene
    D. a paste cleanser made from water and cleaning powder

11. The BEST way to dust desks is to use a
    A. circular motion with soft dry cloth that has been washed
    B. damp cloth, taking care not to disturb papers on the desk
    C. soft cloth, moistened with oil, using a back and forth motion
    D. back and forth motion with a soft dry cloth

12. Trisodium phosphate is a substance BEST used in
    A. washing kalsomined walls
    B. polishing of brass
    C. washing mastic tile floors
    D. clearing stoppages

13. Treated linoleum is PROPERLY cleaned by daily
    A. dusting with a treated mop
    B. sweeping with a floor brush
    C. mopping with a weak soap solution
    D. mopping after removal of dust with a floor brush

14. Of the following, the MOST proper use for chamois skin is
    A. drying of window glass after washing
    B. washing of window glass
    C. polishing of metal fixtures
    D. drying toilet bowls after washing

15. A squeegee is a tool which is used in
    A. clearing stoppage in waste lines
    B. the central vacuum cleaning system
    C. cleaning inside boiler surfaces
    D. drying windows after washing

16. Concrete and cement floors are usually painted a battleship gray color. The MOST important reason for painting the floor is
    A. to improve the appearance of the floor
    B. the paint prevents the absorption of too much water when the floor is mopped
    C. the paint makes the floor safer and less slippery
    D. the concrete becomes harder and will not settle

17. After a sweeping assignment is completed, floor brushes should be stored
    A. in the normal sweeping position, bristles resting on the floor
    B. by hanging the brushes on pegs or nails
    C. by piling the brushes on each other carefully in a horizontal position
    D. in a dry place after a daily washing

18. Painted walls and ceilings should be brushed down
    A. daily
    B. weekly
    C. every month, especially during the winter
    D. two or three times a year

19. If an asphalt tile floor becomes excessively dirty, the method of cleaning should include
    A. the use of kerosene or benzene as a solvent
    B. the use of a solution of modified laundry soda
    C. sanding down the spotted areas with a sanding machine on the wet floor
    D. use of a light oil and treated mop

20. To remove light stains from marble walls, the BEST method is to
    A. use steel wool and a scouring powder, then rinse with clear warm water
    B. wash the stained area with a dilute acid solution
    C. sand down the spot first, then wash with mild soap solution
    D. wet marble first, then scrub with mild soap solution using a soft fiber brush

21. To rid a toilet room of objectionable odors, the PROPER method is to
    A. spread some chloride of lime on the floor
    B. place deodorizer cubes in a box hung on the wall
    C. wash the floor with hot water containing a little kerosene
    D. wash the floor with hot water into which some disinfectant has been poured

22. Toilet rooms, to be cleaned properly, should be swept
    A. daily
    B. and mopped daily
    C. daily and mopped twice a week
    D. daily and mopped thoroughly at the end of the week

23. In waxing a floor, it is usually BEST to
    A. start the waxing under stationary furniture and then do the aisles
    B. pour the wax on the floor, spreading it under the desks with a wax mop
    C. remove the old wax coat before rewaxing
    D. wet mop the floor after the second coat has dried to obtain a high polish

24. The BEST reason why water should not be used to clean kalsomined walls of a boiler room is that the
    A. walls are usually not smooth and will hold too much water
    B. kalsomine coating does not hold dust
    C. kalsomine coating will dissolve in water and leave streaks
    D. wall brick and kalsomine coating will not dissolve in water and so cannot be cleaned

25. In mopping a floor, it is BEST practice to 25.____
    A. swing the mop from side to side, using the widest possible stroke across the floor up to the baseboard
    B. swing the mop from side to side, using the widest possible stroke across the floor surface, stopping the stroke from 3 to 5 inches from baseboards
    C. use short, straight strokes, up and back, stopping the strokes about 5 inches from the baseboard
    D. use short straight strokes, up and back, stopping the strokes at the baseboards

KEY (CORRECT ANSWERS)

1.	B		11.	D
2.	D		12.	C
3.	C		13.	A
4.	A		14.	A
5.	C		15.	D
6.	B		16.	B
7.	C		17.	B
8.	D		18.	D
9.	A		19.	D
10.	A		20.	D

21. D
22. B
23. A
24. C
25. B

28

EXAMINATION SECTION
TEST 1

DIRECTIONS: Each question or incomplete statement is followed by several suggested answers or completions. Select the one that BEST answers the question or completes the statement. *PRINT THE LETTER OF THE CORRECT ANSWER IN THE SPACE AT THE RIGHT.*

1. Of the following daily job in the schedule of a custodian, the one he should do FIRST in the morning is to
    A. hang out the flag
    B. open all doors of the school
    C. fire the boilers
    D. dust the principal's office

    1.____

2. When a school custodian is newly assigned to a building at the start of the school term, his FIRST step should be to
    A. examine the building to determine needed maintenance and repair
    B. meet the principal and discuss plans for operation and maintenance of the building
    C. call a meeting of the teaching and custodial staff to explain his plans for the building
    D. review the records of maintenance and operation left by the previous custodian

    2.____

3. A detergent is a material GENERALLY used for
    A. coating floors to resist water
    B. snow removal
    C. insulation of steam and hot water lines
    D. cleaning purposes

    3.____

4. A good disinfectant is one that will
    A. have a clean odor which will cover up disagreeable odors
    B. destroy germs and create more sanitary conditions
    C. dissolve encrusted dirt and other sources of disagreeable odors
    D. dissolve grease and other materials that may cause stoppage in toilet waste lines

    4.____

5. To help prevent leaks at the joints of water lines, the pipe threads are commonly covered with
    A. tar
    B. cup grease
    C. rubber cement
    D. white lead

    5.____

6. The advantage of using screws instead of nails is that
    A. they have greater holding power
    B. they are available in a greater variety than are nails
    C. a hammer is not required for joining wood members
    D. they are less expensive

    6.____

7. Of the following, the grade of steel wool that is FINEST is
   A. 00   B. 0   C. 1   D. 2

8. The material used with solder to make it stick better is
   A. oakum   B. lye   C. oil   D. flux

9. In using a floor brush in a corridor, a cleaner should be instructed to
   A. use moderately long pull strokes whenever possible
   B. make certain that there is no overlap on sweeping strokes
   C. give the brush a slight jerk after each stroke to free it of loose dirt
   D. keep the sweeping surface of the brush firmly flat on the floor to obtain maximum coverage

10. Of the following, the MOST proper procedure in sweeping classroom floors is to
    A. open all windows before beginning the sweeping operation
    B. move forward while sweeping
    C. alternate pull and push strokes
    D. sweep under desks on both sides of an aisle while moving down the aisle

11. PROPER care of floor brushes includes
    A. washing brushes daily after each use with warm soap solution
    B. dipping brushes in kerosene periodically to remove dirt
    C. washing with warm soap solution at least once a month
    D. avoiding contact with soap or soda solutions to prevent drying of bristles

12. An advantage of vacuum cleaning rather than sweeping a floor with a floor brush is that
    A. stationary furniture will not be touched by the cleaning tool
    B. the problem of dust on furniture is reduced
    C. the initial cost of the apparatus is less than the cost of an equivalent number of floor brushes
    D. daily sweeping of rooms and corridors can be eliminated

13. Sweeping compound for use on rubber tile, asphalt tile or sealed wood floors must NOT contain
    A. sawdust   B. water   C. oil soap   D. floor oil

14. Of the following, the MOST desirable material to use in dusting furniture is a
    A. soft cotton cloth   B. hand towel
    C. counter brush   D. feather duster

15. In high dusting of walls and ceilings, the CORRECT procedure is to
    A. begin with the lower walls and proceed up to the ceiling
    B. remove pictures and window shades only if they are dusty
    C. clean the windows thoroughly before dusting any other part of the room
    D. begin with the ceiling and then dust the walls

16. When cleaning a classroom, the cleaner should
    A. dust desks before sweeping
    B. dust desks after sweeping
    C. open windows during the desk dusting process
    D. begin dusting at rows most distant from the entrance door

17. Too much water on asphalt tile is objectionable MAINLY because the tile
    A. will tend to become discolored or spotted
    B. may be loosened from the floor
    C. will be softened and made uneven
    D. colors will tend to run

18. To reduce the slip hazard resulting from waxing linoleum, the MOST practical of the following methods is to
    A. apply the wax in one heavy coat
    B. apply the wax after varnishing the linoleum
    C. buff the wax surface thoroughly
    D. apply the wax in several thin coats

19. Assume that the water-emulsion was needed for routine waxing in your building is 15 gallons per month. This wax is supplied in 55 gallon drums.
    To cover your needs for a year, the MINIMUM number of drums you would have to request is
    A. two   B. three   C. four   D. six

20. In washing down walls the correct procedure is to start at the bottom of the wall and work to the top.
    The MOST important reason for this is that
    A. dirt streaking will tend to be avoided or easily removed
    B. less cleansing agent will be required
    C. rinse water will not be required
    D. the time for cleaning the wall is less than if washing started at the top of the wall

21. In mopping a wood floor of a classroom, the cleaner should   21.____
    A. mop against the grain of the wood wherever possible
    B. mop as large an area as possible at one time
    C. wet the floor before mopping with a cleaning agent
    D. mop only aisles and clear areas and use a scrub brush under desks and chairs

22. A precaution to observe in mopping asphalt tile floors is:
    A. Keep all pails off such floors because they will leave water marks
    B. Do not wear rubber footwear while mopping those floors
    C. Use circular motion in rinsing and drying the floor to avoid streaking
    D. Never use a cleaning agent containing trisodium phosphate

23. The MOST commonly used cleansing agent for the removal of ink stains 23.____
    from a wood floor is
    A. kerosene   B. oxalic acid
    C. lye   D. bicarbonate soda

24. The FIRST operation in routine cleaning of toilets and washrooms is to 24.____
    A. wash floors   B. clean walls
    C. clean washbasins   D. empty waste receptacles

25. To eliminate the cause of odors in toilet rooms, the tile floors should be 25.____
    mopped with
    A. a mild solution of soap and trisodium phosphate in water
    B. dilute lye solution followed by a hot water rinse
    C. dilute muriatic acid dissolved in hot water
    D. carbon tetrachloride dissolved in hot water

KEY (CORRECT ANSWERS)

1.	C	11.	C
2.	B	12.	B
3.	D	13.	D
4.	B	14.	A
5.	D	15.	D
6.	A	16.	B
7.	A	17.	B
8.	D	18.	D
9.	C	19.	C
10.	B	20.	A

21. C
22. A
23. B
24. D
25. A

TEST 2

DIRECTIONS: Each question or incomplete statement is followed by several suggested answers or completions. Select the one that BEST answers the question or completes the statement. *PRINT THE LETTER OF THE CORRECT ANSWER IN THE SPACE AT THE RIGHT.*

1. The PRINCIPAL reason why soap should NOT be used in cleaning windows is that
    A. it causes loosening of the putty
    B. it may cause rotting of the wood frame
    C. a film is left on the window, requiring additional rinsing
    D. frequent use of soap will cause the glass to become permanently clouded

1.____

2. The CHIEF value of having windows consisting of many small panes of glass is that
    A. the window is much stronger
    B. accident hazards are eliminated
    C. the cost of replacing broken panes is low
    D. cleaning windows consisting of small panes is easier than cleaning a window with a large undivided pane

2.____

3. Cleansing powders such as Ajax should NOT be used to clean and polish brass MAINLY because
    A. the brass turns a much darker color
    B. such cleansers have no effect on tarnish
    C. the surface of the brass may become scratched
    D. too much fine dust is raised in the polishing process

3.____

4. To remove chalk marks on sidewalks and cemented playground areas, the MOST acceptable cleaning method is
    A. using a brush with warm water
    B. using a brush with warm water containing some kerosene
    C. hosing down such areas with water
    D. using a brush with a solution of muriatic acid in water

4.____

5. The MOST important reason for oiling wood floors is that
    A. it keeps the dust from rising during the sweeping process
    B. the need for daily sweeping of classrooms floors is eliminated
    C. oiled floors present a better appearance than waxed floors
    D. the wood surface will become waterproof and stain-proof

5.____

6. After oil has been sprayed on a wood floor, the sprayer should be cleaned before storing it.
    The USUAL cleaning material for this purpose is
    A. ammonia water   B. salt
    C. kerosene   D. alcohol

6.____

7. The MOST desirable agent for routine cleaning of slate blackboards is 7.____
   A. warm water containing trisodium phosphate
   B. mild soap solution in warm water
   C. kerosene in warm water
   D. warm water alone

8. Neatsfoot oil is commonly used to 8.____
   A. oil light machinery
   B. prepare compound
   C. clean metal fixtures
   D. treat leather-covered chairs

Questions 9-12.

DIRECTIONS: Column I lists cleaning agents used by a custodian. Cleaning operations are given in Column II. Select the MOST common cleaning operation for the cleaning agents listed in Column I and print the letter representing your choice next to the number of the agent in the space at the right.

COLUMN I   COLUMN II

9. Ammonia   A. Add to water to clean marble walls 9.____
10. Muriatic acid   B. Remove chewing gum from wood floors 10.____
    C. Wash down calcimined ceilings
    D. Add to water for washing rubber tile floors
11. Carbon tetrachloride   E. Remove rust stains from porcelain 11.____
    F. Cleaning brass
12. Trisodium phosphate 12.____

13. In order to stop a faucet from dripping, the custodian would USUALLY have to replace the 13.____
    A. cap nut   B. seat   C. washer   D. spindle

14. Drinking fountains should be adjusted so that the height of the water stream is about _____ inches. 14.____
    A. 6   B. 3   C. 0   D. 12

15. Before starting up the boilers each morning, the custodian or fireman should make certain that 15.____
    A. all blow-off cocks and valves are open
    B. the water is at a safe level
    C. radiator and uninvent valves are open
    D. the main smoke damper is fully closed

16. If the radiator on a one-pipe heating system rattles or makes noise, the PROBABLE cause is that the 16.____
    A. steam pressure is too high
    B. steam pressure is too low
    C. steam valve is wide open
    D. radiator is air-bound

17. Of the following, the LARGEST size of hard coal is 17.____
    A. chestnut   B. egg   C. stove   D. pea

18. The MAIN purpose of baffle plates in a furnace is to
    A. change the direction of flow of heated gases
    B. retard the burning of gases
    C. increase the combustion ratio of the fuel
    D. prevent the escape of flue gases through furnace openings

    18.____

19. The MAIN difference between a steam header and a steam riser for a given heating system is that the
    A. riser is usually larger than the header
    B. header is larger than the riser
    C. riser is a horizontal line and the header is a vertical line
    D. header is insulated while the riser is not insulated

    19.____

20. The try-cocks of steam boilers are used to
    A. act as safety valves
    B. empty the boiler of water
    C. test steam pressure in the boiler
    D. find the height of water in the boiler

    20.____

21. The MOST important reason for cleaning soot from a boiler is that
    A. soot blocks the passage of steam from the boiler
    B. soot gets into the boiler room and makes it dirty
    C. soot reduces the heating efficiency of a boiler
    D. the pressure of soot is a frequent cause of the cracking of boiler tubes

    21.____

22. Panic bolts are standard equipment in school buildings.
    Their MAIN purpose is to
    A. reduce unauthorized opening of doors and closets
    B. allow for easy opening of exit doors of the building
    C. permit rapid removal of screens from windows of the building
    D. shut storeroom doors automatically to reduce fire hazard

    22.____

23. The term RPM is GENERALLY used in connection with the
    A. speed of ventilating fans   B. water capacity of pipe
    C. heating quality of fuel   D. electrical output of a transformer

    23.____

24. A hacksaw is a light-framed saw MOST commonly used to
    A. cut curved patterns in metal   B. trim edges
    C. cut wood in confined spaces   D. cut metal

    24.____

25. A kilowatt is equal to _____ watts.
    A. 500   B. 2,000   C. 1,500   D. 1,000

    25.____

KEY (CORRECT ANSWERS)

1. C
2. C
3. C
4. A
5. A

6. C
7. D
8. D
9. A
10. E

11. B
12. D
13. C
14. B
15. B

16. D
17. B
18. A
19. B
20. D

21. C
22. B
23. A
24. D
25. D

EXAMINATION SECTION
TEST 1

DIRECTIONS: Each question or incomplete statement is followed by several suggested answers or completions. Select the one that BEST answers the question or completes the statement. *PRINT THE LETTER OF THE CORRECT ANSWER IN THE SPACE AT THE RIGHT.*

1. The BEST of the following substances in which to store used paint brushes is 1.____
   A. gasoline
   B. mineral oil
   C. alcohol
   D. linseed oil

2. A CORRECT statement with respect to the use of a file is: 2.____
   A. The coarser the tooth of a file, the less metal will be removed on each stroke of the file
   B. Files are generally made to cut in one direction only
   C. When a file is used to pry apart materials, light pressure should be maintained
   D. In filing rounded surfaces, the file should rest on the work at all times

3. An ACCEPTABLE material to use on a door to overcome slight sticking to the door jamb is 3.____
   A. tallow candle   B. graphite   C. mineral oil   D. #6 oil

4. The PROPER type of wrench to use on plated or polished pipe is a(n) _____ wrench. 4.____
   A. monkey   B. pipe   C. open end   D. strap

5. Of the following, the room which requires the GREATEST amount of illumination per square foot is the 5.____
   A. library   B. gymnasium   C. auditorium   D. sewing room

6. If one of the electric bulbs in a classroom fails to light up when the switch is snapped, the trouble is MOST likely with the 6.____
   A. switch   B. wiring   C. fuse   D. bulb

7. In general, wood should be fine sanded _____ the grain. 7.____
   A. across   B. diagonal to   C. with   D. circular to

8. The reason for blowing down the water column of a boiler daily is to 8.____
   A. prevent priming or foaming in the boiler
   B. keep the passages above and below the glass clean
   C. remove lime and other mineral matter from boiler feedwater
   D. reduce the possibility of excess steam pressure from building up

9. A CORRECT step in the procedure of blowing down a low pressure boiler is: 9.____
   A. Close return valves before starting to open the blow-off valve
   B. Start the job while the boiler is in operation
   C. Add fresh water rapidly to reach the maximum level
   D. Close blow-off valve when the water reaches the lowest row of tubes

10. To determine if efficient burning of fuel is occurring, the device which is used is a(n) 10.____
    A. orsat apparatus
    B. thermostat
    C. pyrometer
    D. bourdon tube

11. The PROPER tool to use to break up clinkers sticking to the grate is a 11.____
    A. shovel   B. slice bar   C. grate bar   D. rake

12. One of the possible results of closing ash pit doors to regulate draft is 12.____
    A. warping or melting of grates
    B. reduced formation of clinkers
    C. steam will become superheated
    D. live coals will fall into the ash pit

13. Good firing methods require that 13.____
    A. the fire bed be thick enough to prevent air from passing through
    B. each side of the grate be kept bare to allow cool air to reach the stack
    C. live coals should not be allowed to burn beneath the grates
    D. the fire be stirred every hour to reduce the amount of unburned gases

14. Of the following, the one that is CORRECT with respect to the burning of hard coal is: 14.____
    A. To prevent clinkers, a hard coal fire should never be poked
    B. The fire bed should not be more than 6 inches thick at any time
    C. Air holes in the bed should be made with a rake or slice bar
    D. Infrequent heavy firing will reduce the possibility of forming holes

15. The MAIN purpose of a Hartford Loop as a return connection for a steam boiler is to 15.____
    A. remove air from the return lines
    B. prevent a boiler from losing its water
    C. allow reduction in boiler header size
    D. reduce friction in return lines

16. If a boiler fails to deliver enough heat, the MOST probable of the following reasons is the 16.____
    A. leaking of the boiler manhole
    B. boiler operating at excessive output
    C. heating surface is covered with soot
    D. unsteady water line as shown by the gauge glass

17. Generally, thermostatic traps of radiators are used to
    A. prevent the flow of water and air and allow the passage of steam
    B. prevent the passage of steam and allow the passage of water and air
    C. stop air from entering the radiator to prevent it from becoming air-bound
    D. relieve the radiator of excess steam if pressure rises too high

18. When a heating boiler is in operation, the safety valve should be tested
    A. semi-annually   B. weekly
    C. monthly   D. whenever it seems to be stuck

19. In the horizontal rotary cup oil burner, the MAIN purpose of the rotary cup is to
    A. provide air for ignition of the oil
    B. pump oil into the burner
    C. atomize the oil into small drops
    D. turn the flame in a circle to heat the furnace walls evenly

20. The BEST reason for having gaskets on manholes of a boiler is to
    A. prevent leakage from the boiler
    B. provide emergency exit for excessive steam pressure
    C. provide easy access to the boiler for cleaning
    D. prevent corrosion at manholes

21. The MAIN purpose of expansion joints in steam lines is to
    A. provide for changes in length of heated pipe
    B. allow for connection of additional radiators
    C. provide locations for valves
    D. reduce breakage of pipe due to minor movement in the building

22. If too much water is put in a boiler, the result will be
    A. excessive smoke   B. excessive rate of steam output
    C. excessive fuel consumption   D. unsteady water line

23. Piping that carries condensate and air from radiators of a heating system is called
    A. dry return if above boiler water line
    B. drip line
    C. wet return if above boiler water line
    D. riser runout

24. Suppose a boiler smokes through the fire door.
    Of the following, the LEAST likely cause is
    A. dirty or clogged flues   B. inferior fuel
    C. defective chimney draft   D. air leaks into boiler

25. Of the following, the statement concerning accident prevention that is NOT correct is: 25.____
    A. Ladders should be unpainted
    B. Remove finger rings before beginning to mop
    C. Wear loose-fitting clothes when working around boilers or machinery
    D. Set ladder bottom at about 1/5 the ladder length away from the wall against which the ladder rests

---

KEY (CORRECT ANSWERS)

1.	D		11.	B
2.	B		12.	A
3.	A		13.	C
4.	D		14.	A
5.	D		15.	B
6.	D		16.	C
7.	C		17.	B
8.	B		18.	B
9.	B		19.	C
10.	A		20.	A

21.
22. C
23. A
24. D
25. C

TEST 2

DIRECTIONS: Each question or incomplete statement is followed by several suggested answers or completions. Select the one that BEST answers the question or completes the statement. *PRINT THE LETTER OF THE CORRECT ANSWER IN THE SPACE AT THE RIGHT.*

1. When the oil burner reset button is pressed, the burner motor does not work. The FIRST thing to check is the
   A. oil supply in oil tanks
   B. possibility of a blown fuse
   C. oil strainers which may be clogged
   D. dirty stack switch

   1.____

2. When a heating plant is laid up for the summer, one of the steps the fireman should take with respect to the boiler is to tap the brace and stay rods with a hammer.
   The MAIN reason for this is to
   A. clean these parts of accumulated rust and dirt
   B. make certain these parts are in place and not out of line
   C. remove them for storage during summer and early autumn seasons
   D. make certain they are tight and not broken

   2.____

3. In the event of a bomb threat, the custodian should take the precaution to
   A. open ash pit and fire doors of boilers
   B. pull the main switch to cut off all power in the building
   C. operate with the least number of water services possible
   D. empty water from boilers immediately after covering fire with ashes

   3.____

4. The type of fire extinguisher that requires protection against freezing is
   A. carbon dioxide   B. carbon tetrachloride (pyrene)
   C. soda acid   D. calcium chloride

   4.____

5. A CORRECT procedure in recharging soda acid fire extinguishers is:
   A. The soda charge should be completely dissolved in 28 gallons of boiling water
   B. The filled acid bottle should be tightly stoppered before it is placed back in the extinguisher
   C. The extinguisher must be recharged after use regardless of extent of use
   D. Be sure to fill container with soda solution to the top of container up to threads of cap

   5.____

6. The MOST common cause of slipperiness of a terrazzo floor after being washed is the
   A. failure to rinse floor clean after cleaning agent is used
   B. destruction of floor seal by cleaning agent
   C. incomplete removal of dirt from the floor
   D. use of oil in the cleaning process

   6.____

7. When electric lighting fixtures are washed, a precaution to observe is that 7.____
   A. the metal part of the fixture should be washed with a warm mild ammonia solution
   B. the holding screws of glass globes should be loosened about half a turn after cleaning globes
   C. trisodium phosphate should not be used in washing glass globes because it dulls glass
   D. chain links of fixture should be loosened to enable removal of entire fixture

8. Inside burns on recently cut pipe are USUALLY removed by 8.____
   A. filing   B. turning   C. reaming   D. sanding

9. When the average temperature for a day is 48°F, the number of degree days for that day is 9.____
   A. 22   B. 27   C. 12   D. 17

10. Water hammer will MOST likely occur in the 10.____
    A. self-closing valves of a drinking fountain
    B. bends in a pipe line where air can accumulate
    C. globe valve on the supply line to a fixture
    D. angle valve on the steam supply line to a radiator

11. To remove a stoppage in a trap which has not cleared by the use of a force cup, the tool to use is a(n) 11.____
    A. yarning tool   B. auger
    C. expansion bit   D. trowel

12. If the float of a flush tank leaks and fills with water, the MOST probable result will be 12.____
    A. no water in the tank   B. ball cock remains open
    C. water will flow over the tank rim   D. flush ball will not seat properly

13. Fresh air inlets are GENERALLY installed in connection with a 13.____
    A. house trap   B. roof vent
    C. sump pump   D. branch soil pipe

14. The PRIMARY function of the water trap in the waste line from a wash bowl is to 14.____
    A. hold excess water from flooding waste line
    B. prevent the flow of sewer gas into the room
    C. catch particles and refuse that may enter the line with the water
    D. provide an easy means for cleaning and repairing the waste line

15. The BEST lubricant for a cylinder lock is 15.____
    A. crude oil   B. machine oil   C. tallow   D. graphite

16. A window sash holds the
    A. casing B. glass C. jambs D. sills

17. The BEST procedure to follow to determine the actual cleaning ability of a specific material is to
    A. test its performance
    B. read the specifications
    C. ask the manufacturer
    D. examine trade literature

Questions 18-21.

DIRECTIONS: Questions 18 through 21 are to be answered on the basis of the following occurrence.

An accident occurred at P.S. 947 on Monday, January 14, resulting in the injury of a fireman-cleaner named John Jones. Jones was found unconscious on the floor of the boiler room. He showed evidence of a head injury. An ambulance was called immediately. Jones was treated by the ambulance attendant, who found no serious injury and treated the head wound. Jones, when asked about the cause of the injury, stated that he had fallen over a coal shovel lying in his path. The head injury apparently resulted from the hard contact of Jones' head with a concrete post. Jones was then taken home and was advised to check with a doctor if he felt groggy or ill. An examination of the boiler room revealed that an electric light located near the scene of the accident was out and that the area was quite dark. There were no witnesses to the accident.

18. Of the following, the information MOST necessary to make the required report on the accident is
    A. Jones' age
    B. Jones' work habits
    C. the name of the person who found Jones injured
    D. whether Jones was covered by Workmen's Compensation

19. When Jones was found, a safety precaution that should have been taken was
    A. extinguishing the fire in the furnace
    B. the removal of Jones to a place where the lighting was more satisfactory
    C. avoiding movement of Jones to prevent further injury
    D. raising Jones' head to restore him to consciousness

20. In accordance with Workmen's Compensation regulations, Jones has the right to
    A. compensation if his injuries keep him from work more than one week
    B. use any doctor provided the doctor is approved by the custodian
    C. compensation greater than the amount of his wages if he is seriously injured
    D. compensation only if he proves he did not place the shovel where it was found

21. The MOST important lesson that the custodian should learn from this accident is that
    A. before an employee starts work, his place of work should be inspected by the custodian
    B. even experienced firemen-cleaners require regular weekly training in the proper performance of their duties
    C. employee should be required to turn in old burned-out electric bulb before receiving new ones
    D. regular inspections of work spaces are required to reduce accidents to a minimum

22. Information which is of the LEAST value in a report of unlawful entry into a school building is the
    A. estimated value of missing property
    B. means of entry
    C. time and date of entry
    D. general description of the school building

23. You notice several children marking an entrance door with chalk. The MOST desirable immediate action to take is to
    A. stop the children and tell them not to do this again
    B. ask the principal to stop the children from defacing the door
    C. take the names of the children and write to their parents
    D. remove the chalk marks, but say nothing to the children

24. Suppose that the principal advises you that there are peddlers selling their wares at sidewalk locations surrounding the school premises. The MOST appropriate action to take FIRST is to
    A. put up signs warning the peddlers that they are violating the law
    B. advise the peddlers that such activity on sidewalks of the school is illegal and to move on
    C. call the police immediately to clear the sidewalks
    D. suggest that the teachers tell their pupils not to patronize these unsupervised peddlers

25. A parent complains that her child refuses to use the school toilet because it is unclean. The FIRST step you should take upon receipt of the complaint from the school principal is to
    A. advise the principal that the toilets are kept clean and that the complaint is unwarranted
    B. tell the cleaner in charge of the floor on which the toilet is located to clean the toilet properly
    C. visit the school toilets to check on the statement made in the complaint
    D. ask the parent to see the toilets for herself rather than take the word of her child

KEY (CORRECT ANSWERS)

1. B
2. D
3. C
4. C
5. C

6. A
7. B
8. C
9. D
10. A

11. B
12. B
13. A
14. B
15. D

16. B
17. A
18. C
19. C
20. A

21. D
22. D
23. A
24. B
25. C

46

EXAMINATION SECTION
TEST 1

DIRECTIONS: Each question or incomplete statement is followed by several suggested answers or completions. Select the one that BEST answers the question or completes the statement. *PRINT THE LETTER OF THE CORRECT ANSWER IN THE SPACE AT THE RIGHT.*

1. Before starting any lawn mowing, the distance between the blade and a flat surface should be measured with a ruler. This distance should be such that the cut of the grass above the ground is _____ inch(es).

    A. 1   B. 1 1/2   C. 2   D. 3

2. Strainers in a number 6 fuel oil system should be checked once a

    A. day   B. week   C. month   D. year

3. The spinning cup on a rotary cup oil burner should be cleaned once

    A. a day
    B. a week
    C. every two weeks
    D. a month

4. Terrazzo floors should be cleaned daily with a

    A. damp mop using clear water
    B. damp mop using a strong alkaline solution
    C. damp mop using a mild acid solution
    D. dust mop treated with vegetable oil

5. New installations of vinyl-asbestos floors should

    A. never be machine scrubbed
    B. be dry-buffed weekly
    C. be swept daily, using an oily compound
    D. never be swept with treated dust mops

6. Standpipe fire hose shall be inspected

    A. monthly
    B. quarterly
    C. semi-annually
    D. annually

7. All portable fire extinguishers shall be inspected once

    A. a year
    B. a month
    C. a week
    D. every 3 months

8. Soda-acid and foam-type fire extinguishers shall be discharged and recharged at least once

    A. each year
    B. every two years
    C. every six months
    D. each month

9. Elevator *safeties* under the car shall be tested once each

    A. day   B. week   C. month   D. quarter

10. Key-type fire alarms in public school buildings shall be tested

    A. daily
    B. weekly
    C. monthly
    D. quarterly

11. Combustion efficiency can be determined from an appropriate chart used in conjunction with _____ temperature and

    A. steam; steam pressure
    B. flue gas; percentage of CO_2
    C. flue gas; fuel heating value
    D. oil; steam pressure

12. In the combustion of common fuels, the major boiler heat loss is due to

    A. incomplete combustion
    B. moisture in the fuel
    C. heat radiation
    D. heat lost in the flue gases

13. The MOST important reason for blowing down a boiler water column and gauge glass is to

    A. prevent the gauge glass level from rising too high
    B. relieve stresses in the gauge glass
    C. insure a true water level reading
    D. insure a true pressure gauge reading

14. The secondary voltage of a transformer used for ignition in a fuel oil burner has a range of MOST NEARLY _____ volts to _____ volts.

    A. 120; 240
    B. 440; 660
    C. 660; 1,200
    D. 5,000; 15,000

15. Assume that during the month of April there were 3 days with an average outdoor temperature of 30° F, 7 days with 40° F, 10 days with 50° F, 3 days with 60° F, and 7 days with 65° F.
    The number of degree days for the month was

    A. 330
    B. 445
    C. 595
    D. 1,150

16. The pH of boiler feedwater is usually maintained within the range of

    A. 4 to 5
    B. 6 to 7
    C. 10 to 12
    D. 13 to 14

17. The admission of steam to the coils of a domestic hot water supply tank is regulated by a(n)

    A. pressure regulating valve
    B. immersion type temperature gauge
    C. check valve
    D. thermostatic control valve

18. The device which senses primary air failure in a rotary cup oil burner is usually called a(n)   18.____

    A. vaporstat   B. anemometer
    C. venturi   D. pressure gauge

19. The device which starts and stops the flow of oil into an automatic rotary cup oil burner is usually called a(n) _____ valve.   19.____

    A. magnetic oil   B. oil metering
    C. oil check   D. relief

20. A vacuum breaker, used on a steam heated domestic hot water tank, is usually connected to the   20.____

    A. circulating pump   B. tank wall
    C. aquastat   D. steam coil flange

21. A vacuum pump in a low pressure steam heating system which is equipped with a float switch, a vacuum switch, a magnetic starter, and a selector switch can be operated on   21.____

    A. float, vacuum, or automatic
    B. float, vacuum, or continuous
    C. vacuum, automatic, or continuous
    D. float, automatic, or continuous

22. If the temperature of the condensate returning to the vacuum pump in a low pressure steam vacuum heating system is above 180° F, the trouble may be caused by   22.____

    A. faulty radiator traps
    B. room thermostats being set too high
    C. uninsulated return lines
    D. too many radiators being shut off

23. A feedwater regulator operates to   23.____

    A. shut down the burner when the water is low
    B. maintain the water in the boiler at a predetermined level
    C. drain the water from the boiler
    D. regulate the temperature of the feedwater

24. An automatically fired steam boiler is equipped with an automatic low water cut-off. The low water cut-off is usually actuated by   24.____

    A. steam pressure   B. fuel pressure
    C. float action   D. water temperature

25. Low pressure steam or an electric heater is usually required for heating No. _____ fuel oil.   25.____

    A. 1   B. 2   C. 4   D. 6

KEY (CORRECT ANSWERS)

1.	C	11.	B
2.	A	12.	D
3.	A	13.	C
4.	A	14.	D
5.	B	15.	B
6.	B	16.	C
7.	B	17.	D
8.	A	18.	A
9.	C	19.	A
10.	A	20.	D

21. D
22. A
23. B
24. C
25. D

TEST 2

DIRECTIONS: Each question or incomplete statement is followed by several suggested answers or completions. Select the one that BEST answers the question or completes the statement. *PRINT THE LETTER OF THE CORRECT ANSWER IN THE SPACE AT THE RIGHT.*

1. A compound gauge is calibrated to read

    A. pressure only
    B. vacuum only
    C. vacuum and pressure
    D. temperature and humidity

    1.____

2. In a mechanical pressure-atomizing type oil burner, the oil is atomized by using an atomizing tip and

    A. steam pressure
    B. pump pressure
    C. compressed air
    D. a spinning cup

    2.____

3. A good over-the-fire draft in a natural draft furnace should be approximately _____ inches of water _____.

    A. 5.0; positive pressure
    B. 0.05; positive pressure
    C. 0.05; vacuum
    D. 5.0; vacuum

    3.____

4. When it is necessary to add chemicals to a heating boiler, it should be done

    A. immediately after boiler blowdown
    B. after the boiler has been cleaned internally of sludge, scale, and other foreign matter
    C. at periods when condensate flow to the boiler is small
    D. at a time when there is a heavy flow of condensate to the boiler

    4.____

5. The modutrol motor on a rotary cup oil burner burning #6 fuel oil automatically operates the primary air damper,

    A. secondary air damper, and oil metering valve
    B. secondary air damper, and magnetic oil valve
    C. oil metering valve, and magnetic oil valve
    D. and magnetic oil valve

    5.____

6. The manual-reset pressuretrol is classified as a _____ Control.

    A. Safety and Operating
    B. Limit and Operating
    C. Limit and Safety
    D. Limit, Operating, and Safety

    6.____

7. Sodium sulphite is added to boiler feedwater to

    A. avoid caustic embrittlement
    B. increase the pH value
    C. reduce the tendency of foaming in the steam drum
    D. remove dissolved oxygen

    7.____

51

8. Neat cement is a mixture of cement,

   A. putty, and water B. and water
   C. lime and water   D. salt, and water

9. In a concrete mix of 1:2:4, the 2 refers to the amount of

   A. sand   B. cement   C. stone   D. water

10. The word *natatorium* means MOST NEARLY a(n)

    A. auditorium   B. playroom
    C. gymnasium   D. indoor swimming pool

11. Plated metal surfaces which are protected by a thin coat of clear lacquer should be cleaned with a(n)

    A. abrasive compound   B. liquid polish
    C. mild soap solution   D. lemon oil solution

12. Wet mop filler replacements are ordered by

    A. length   B. weight
    C. number of strands   D. trade number

13. The BEST way to determine the value of a cleaning material is by

    A. performance testing
    B. manufacturer's literature
    C. written specifications
    D. interviews with manufacturer's salesman

14. The instructions on a container of cleaning compound states, *Mix one pound of compound in 5 gallons of water.* Using these instructions, the amount of compound which should be added to 15 quarts of water is MOST likely _____ ounces.

    A. 3   B. 8   C. 12   D. 48

15. The MOST usual cause of paint blisters is

    A. too much oil in the paint
    B. moisture under the paint coat
    C. a heavy coat of paint
    D. improper drying of the paint

16. The floor that should NOT be machined scrubbed is a(n)

    A. lobby   B. lunchroom
    C. gymnasium   D. auditorium aisle

17. Pick-up sweeping in a school building is the occasional removal of the more conspicuous loose dirt from corridors and lobbies.
    This type of sweeping should be done

    A. after scrubbing or waxing of floors
    B. with the aid of a sweeping compound
    C. at night after school hours
    D. during regular school hours

18. According to recommended practice, when a steam boiler is taken out of service for a long period of time, the boiler drums should FIRST be

    A. drained completely while the water is hot (above 212° F)
    B. drained completely after the water has been cooled down to 180° F
    C. filled completely without draining
    D. filled to the level of the top try cock

19. Specifications concerning window cleaners' anchors and safety belts must be in compliance with the rules and regulations outlined in the

    A. State Labor Law and Board of Standards and Appeals
    B. Building Code
    C. Fire Department Safety Manual
    D. National Protection Association

20. If it is not possible to plant new shrubs immediately upon delivery in the spring, they should be stored in a(n)

    A. sheltered outdoor area
    B. unsheltered outdoor area
    C. boiler room
    D. warm place indoors

21. Peat moss is generally used for its

    A. food value
    B. nitrogen
    C. alkalinity
    D. moisture retaining quality

22. The legal minimum age of employees engaged for cleaning windows in the state is _____ years.

    A. 16   B. 17   C. 18   D. 21

23. Pruning of street trees is the responsibility of the

    A. School Custodian Engineer
    B. Board of Education
    C. Department of Parks
    D. Borough President's Office

24. The prevention and control of vermin and rodents in a school building is PRIMARILY a matter of

    A. maintaining good housekeeping on a continuous basis
    B. periodic use of an exterminator's service
    C. calling in the exterminator when necessary
    D. cleaning the building thoroughly during school vacation

25. The MAIN classification of lumber used for construction purposes is known as _____ lumber.

    A. industrial
    B. commercial
    C. finish
    D. yard

KEY (CORRECT ANSWERS)

1. C
2. B
3. C
4. D
5. A

6. C
7. D
8. B
9. A
10. D

11. C
12. B
13. A
14. C
15. B

16. C
17. D
18. B
19. A
20. A

21. D
22. C
23. C
24. A
25. D

TEST 3

DIRECTIONS: Each question or incomplete statement is followed by several suggested answers or completions. Select the one that BEST answers the question or completes the statement. *PRINT THE LETTER OF THE CORRECT ANSWER IN THE SPACE AT THE RIGHT.*

1. Oil-soaked waste and rags should be 1.____

    A. deposited in a self-closing metal can
    B. piled in the open
    C. stored in the supply closet
    D. rolled up and be available for the next job

2. Inspection for safety should be included as part of the custodian engineer's _____ inspection. 2.____

    A. daily   B. weekly   C. monthly   D. quarterly

3. Of the following classifications, the one which pertains to fires in electrical equipment is Class 3.____

    A. A   B. B   C. C   D. D

4. The type of portable fire extinguisher which is PARTICULARLY suited for extinguishing flammable liquid fires is the _____ type. 4.____

    A. soda-acid   B. foam
    C. pump tank   D. loaded stream

5. Of the following liquids, the one which has the LOWEST flash point is 5.____

    A. kerosene   B. gasoline
    C. benzene   D. carbon tetrachloride

6. When giving first aid to an injured person, which one of the following should you NOT do? 6.____

    A. Administer medication internally
    B. Send for a physician
    C. Control bleeding
    D. Treat for shock

7. In reference to firefighting, fires are of such complexity that 7.____

    A. no plans or methods of attack can be formulated in advance
    B. the problem must be considered in advance and methods of attack formulated
    C. an appointed committee is necessary to direct fighting at the fire
    D. no planned procedures can be relied on

8. The heat of a soldering copper should be tested 8.____

    A. with solder
    B. by holding it near kraft paper
    C. by holding it near your hand
    D. with water

9. Safety on the job is BEST assured by

    A. keeping alert
    B. following every rule
    C. working very slowly
    D. never working alone

10. One important use of accident reports is to provide information that may be used to reduce the possibility of similar accidents.
    The MOST valuable entry on the report for this purpose is the

    A. time lost due to accident
    B. date of the occurrence
    C. injury sustained by the victim
    D. cause of the accident

11. If the directions given by your superior are NOT clear, the BEST thing for you to do is to

    A. ask to have the directions repeated and clarified
    B. proceed to do the work taking a chance on doing the right thing
    C. do nothing until some later time when you can find out exactly what is wanted
    D. ask one of the other men in your crew what he would do under the circumstances

12. Of the following procedures concerning grievances of subordinate personnel, the custodian engineer should maintain an attitude of

    A. paying little attention to little grievances
    B. being very alert to grievances and make adjustments in existing conditions to appease all personnel
    C. knowing the most frequent causes of grievances and strive to prevent them from arising
    D. maintaining rigid discipline of a nature that *smooths out* all grievances

13. Of the following, the BEST course of action to take to settle a dispute or conflict between two employees is to

    A. insist that the two employees settle the case between themselves
    B. call in each one separately and after hearing their cases presented, decide the issue
    C. bring both in for a conference at the same time and make the decision in their presence
    D. have both present their points of view and arguments in a written memoranda and on this basis make your decision

14. If, as a custodian engineer, you discover an error in your report submitted to the main office, you should

    A. do nothing, since it is possible that one error will have little effect on the total report
    B. wait until the error is discovered in the main office and then offer to work overtime to correct it
    C. go directly to the supervisor in the main office after working hours and ask him unofficially to correct the error
    D. notify the main office immediately so that the error can be corrected, if necessary

15. There are a considerable number of forms and reports to be submitted on schedule by the custodian engineer. The advisable method of accomplishing this duty is to

    A. fill out the reports at odd times during the days when you have free time
    B. schedule a definite period of the work week for completing these forms and reports
    C. assign your foreman or cleaner to handle all these forms for you and to have them available on time
    D. classify or group the forms and reports and fill out only one of each group and refer the other forms or reports to the ones completed

16. A custodian engineer can BEST evaluate the quality of work performed by custodial personnel by

    A. periodic inspection of the building's cleanliness
    B. studying the time records of personnel
    C. reviewing the building cleaning expenditures
    D. analyzing complaints of building occupants

17. Assume that you are the custodian engineer and one of your employees wants to talk with you about a grievance. Of the following actions, the LEAST desirable action for you to take is to

    A. listen sympathetically
    B. conduct the discussion openly in the presence of the workforce
    C. try to get his point of view
    D. endeavor to obtain all the facts

18. Of the following factors, the one which is LEAST important in evaluating an employee and his work is his

    A. dependability   B. quantity of work done
    C. quality of work done   D. education and training

19. Supervision of a group of people engaged in building cleaning operations should NOT include supervision of

    A. time spent in cleaning operations
    B. utilization of official rest and lunch periods
    C. cleaning methods
    D. materials used for various cleaning jobs

20. Of the following methods, the BEST one to utilize in assigning custodial personnel to clean a multi-floor school building is to

    A. allow the cleaners to pick their room or area assignments out of a hat
    B. have the supervisor make specific room or area assignments to each cleaner separately
    C. rotate room and area assignments daily according to a chart posted on the bulletin board
    D. let a different member of the group make the room or area assignments each week

21. Assume that you are the custodian engineer and that you have discovered a bottle of liquor in one of your employee's locker.
The BEST course of action to take is to

    A. fire him immediately
    B. explain to him that liquor should not be brought into a school building and that a repetition may result
    C. in disciplinary action
    D. suspend him until the end of the week and take him back only on a probational basis
    E. assemble the staff and tell them they are all equally guilty for not having reported the matter to you

22. Of the following items, the one which is the LEAST important in the preparation of a report is that the report

    A. is brief, but to the point
    B. uses the prescribed form if there is one
    C. contains extra copies
    D. is accurate

23. In order to have building employees willing to follow standardized cleaning and maintenance procedures, the supervisor must be prepared to

    A. work alongside the employees
    B. demonstrate the reasonableness of the procedures
    C. offer incentive pay for their utilization
    D. allow the employees the free use of the time saved by their adoption

24. Suppose that you are the custodian engineer and one of your employees has gross earnings of $437.10 for the week, all of which is subject to deductions at the rate of 4.8%. The amount which should be deducted from the employee's gross earnings for the week is MOST NEARLY

    A. $2.10   B. $14.70   C. $17.70   D. $20.97

25. Suppose that you are a custodian engineer and an employee works for you at the rate of $8.70 per hour with time and one-half paid for time worked after 40 hours in one week. His gross pay for working 53 hours in one week is MOST NEARLY

    A. $461.10   B. $482.10   C. $487.65   D. $517.65

KEY (CORRECT ANSWERS)

1. A
2. A
3. C
4. B
5. B

6. A
7. B
8. A
9. A
10. D

11. A
12. C
13. C
14. D
15. B

16. A
17. B
18. D
19. B
20. B

21. B
22. C
23. B
24. D
25. D

TEST 4

DIRECTIONS: Each question or incomplete statement is followed by several suggested answers or completions. Select the one that BEST answers the question or completes the statement. *PRINT THE LETTER OF THE CORRECT ANSWER IN THE SPACE AT THE RIGHT.*

1. The minimum number of gate valves usually required in a by-pass around a steam trap is   1._____

   A. 1   B. 2   C. 3   D. 4

2. A 2-inch standard steel pipe, as compared with a 2-inch extra heavy steel pipe, has the same   2._____

   A. wall thickness   B. inside diameter
   C. outside diameter   D. weight per linear foot

3. A short piece of pipe with a standard male pipe thread on one end and a locknut thread on the other end is usually called a   3._____

   A. close nipple   B. tank nipple
   C. coupling   D. union

4. Dies are used by plumbers to   4._____

   A. ream out the inside of pipes
   B. thread pipes
   C. bevel the ends of pipes
   D. make up solder joints

5. Of the following types of pipe, the one which is MOST brittle is   5._____

   A. brass   B. copper
   C. cast iron   D. wrought iron

6. The PRIMARY function of a trap in a drainage system is   6._____

   A. prevent gases from flowing into the building
   B. produce an efficient flushing action
   C. prevent articles accidentally dropped into the drainage system from entering the water
   D. prevent the water backing up

7. If a plumbing fixture is allowed to stand unused for a long time, its trap is opt to lose its seal by   7._____

   A. evaporation   B. capillary action
   C. siphonage   D. condensation

8. The pipe fitting used to connect a 1 1/4" pipe directly to a 1" pipe in a straight line is called a   8._____

   A. union   B. nipple   C. elbow   D. reducer

9. The BEST procedure to follow when replacing a blown fuse is to

    A. immediately replace it with the same size fuse
    B. immediately replace it with a larger size fuse
    C. immediately replace it with a smaller size fuse
    D. correct the cause of the fuse failure and replace it with the correct size

10. The amperage rating of the fuse to be used in an electrical circuit is determined by the

    A. size of the connected load
    B. size of the wire in the circuit
    C. voltage of the circuit
    D. ambient temperature

11. In a 208-volt, 3-phase, 4-wire circuit, the voltage, in volts, from any line to the grounded neutral is approximately

    A. 208   B. 150   C. 120   D. zero

12. The device commonly used to change an A.C. voltage to a D.C. voltage is called a

    A. transformer   B. rectifier
    C. relay   D. capacitor or condenser

13. Where conduit enters a knock-out in an outlet box, it should be provided with a

    A. bushing on the inside and locknut on the outside
    B. locknut on the inside and bushing on the outside
    C. union on the outside and a nipple on the inside
    D. nipple on the outside and a union on the inside

14. The electric circuit to a ten kilowatt electric hot water heater which is automatically controlled by an aquastat will also require a

    A. transistor   B. choke coil
    C. magnetic contactor   D. limit switch

15. An electric power consumption meter usually indicates the power used in

    A. watts   B. volt-hours
    C. amperes   D. kilowatt-hours

16. Of the following sizes of copper wire, the one which can SAFELY carry the GREATEST amount of amperes is

    A. 14 ga. stranded   B. 12 ga. stranded
    C. 12 ga. solid   D. 10 ga. solid

17. A flexible coupling is PRIMARILY used to

    A. allow for imperfect alignment of two joining shafts
    B. allow for slight differences in shaft diameters
    C. insure perfect alignment of the joining shafts
    D. reduce fast starting of the machinery

18. The one of the following statements concerning lubricating oil which is CORRECT is:

    A. SAE 10 is heavier and more viscous than SAE 30
    B. diluting lubricating oil with gasoline increases its viscosity
    C. oil reduces friction between moving parts
    D. in hot weather, thin oil is preferable to heavy oil

19. The MAIN purpose of periodic inspections and tests made on mechanical equipment is to

    A. make the operating men familiar with the equipment
    B. keep the maintenance men busy during otherwise slack periods
    C. discover minor faults before they develop into serious breakdowns
    D. encourage the men to take better care of the equipment

20. The one of the following bearing types which is NOT classified as a roller bearing is

    A. radial   B. angular   C. thrust   D. babbit

21. In a wire rope, when a number of wires are laid left-handed into a strand and the strand laid right-handed around a hemp rope center, the wire rope is commonly known as a _____ rope.

    A. right-lay, Lang-lay   B. left-lay, Lang-lay
    C. left-lay, regular-lay   D. right-lay, regular-lay

22. The chemical which is NOT used for disinfecting swimming pools is

    A. ammonia   B. calcium hypochlorite
    C. chlorine   D. liquified chlorine

23. The one of the following V-belt sections which has the HIGHEST horsepower-per-belt rating is _____ section.

    A. A   B. B   C. C   D. D

24. An air compressor which is driven by an electric motor is usually started and stopped automatically by a(n)

    A. unloader   B. pressure regulator valve
    C. float switch   D. pressure switch

25. The volume, in cubic feet, of a cylindrical tank, 6 ft. in diameter x 35 ft. long is MOST NEARLY

    A. 210   B. 990   C. 1,260   D. 3,960

KEY (CORRECT ANSWERS)

1. C
2. C
3. B
4. B
5. C

6. A
7. A
8. D
9. D
10. B

11. C
12. B
13. A
14. C
15. D

16. D
17. A
18. C
19. C
20. D

21. D
22. A
23. D
24. D
25. B

EXAMINATION SECTION
TEST 1

DIRECTIONS: Each question or incomplete statement is followed by several suggested answers or completions. Select the one that BEST answers the question or completes the statement. *PRINT THE LETTER OF THE CORRECT ANSWER IN THE SPACE AT THE RIGHT.*

1. An electrical device whose function is to keep boiler steam pressure from exceeding the predetermined pressure is the

   A. relief valve
   B. vaporstat
   C. pressure gage
   D. pressuretrol

   1.____

2. Sodium sulphite is used to

   A. treat boiler water
   B. detect leaks in a gas system
   C. remove ink stains
   D. seal wood

   2.____

3. Boiler water should have a pH value between

   A. 5 and 7   B. 9 and 11   C. 13 and 14   D. 15 and 17

   3.____

4. The percentage of dryness of steam is called steam

   A. purity   B. ratio   C. priming   D. quality

   4.____

5. A bottom blowdown on a boiler is used to

   A. decrease the amount of fuel consumed
   B. increase the boiler steam pressure
   C. decrease the water intake
   D. eliminate impurities from the mud drum

   5.____

6. The flow of oil to a rotary cup oil burner is generally controlled by a(n)

   A. aquastat
   B. steam coil
   C. solenoid valve
   D. venturi

   6.____

7. The unit of a rotary cup oil burner that senses primary air failure is the

   A. remote switch
   B. modutrol
   C. vaporstat
   D. stackmeter

   7.____

8. The quantity of water delivered by a centrifugal pump varies _____ pump speed.

   A. directly as the cube of the
   B. directly as the square of the
   C. directly as the
   D. inversely as the

   8.____

9. The volute casing of a centrifugal pump serves the MAIN purpose of

   A. a priming chamber
   B. venting the pump head
   C. converting velocity head into pressure head
   D. making the pump run quieter

   9.____

65

10. The amount of water vapor mixed with dry air in the atmosphere is known as

   A. saturation ratio
   B. humidity
   C. vapor density
   D. dew point

11. When water freezes at 32° F, the amount of heat lost, per lb. of water is _____ BTU.

   A. 212   B. 180   C. 144   D. 100

12. The one of the following factors which does NOT affect human comfort in air conditioning is air

   A. temperature
   B. purity
   C. motion
   D. absorption

13. The element of a mechanical compression refrigerating system in which the refrigerant absorbs heat is the

   A. evaporator
   B. receiver
   C. condenser
   D. carnot

14. When the water level in a boiler falls below a specified level, the oil burner is shut off by the action of a

   A. magnetic gas valve
   B. purge control
   C. low water cut-out
   D. bellows feed

15. A small by-pass line would be installed around a large gate valve in a water line in order to

   A. measure the flow accurately
   B. show the direction of the flow
   C. alter the liquid flow in case of valve failure
   D. make it easier to open the gate valve

16. Flanged butterfly valves are operated by bringing them from closed to full-open position in _____ turn(s).

   A. 3 full
   B. 2 full
   C. one-half
   D. one-quarter

17. A monometer measures

   A. electrical energy
   B. revolutions per minute
   C. difference in pressure
   D. fluid volume

18. The difference between a compound gage and a standard gage is that the compound gage measures

   A. only pressures less than atmospheric
   B. pressures above and below atmospheric
   C. only pressures greater than atmospheric
   D. only pressures greater than absolute

19. The absolute pressure indicated by a gage reading of 14 psi is *approximately* _____ psi.

   A. 18.0   B. 24.0   C. 28.0   D. 32.0

20. A boiler steam gage should be graduated so that, when indicating the normal operating pressure, its pointer is nearly

   A. horizontal
   B. vertical
   C. 45 off the vertical position
   D. 60 off the vertical position

21. The packing generally used in the expansion points of a firebrick wall is

   A. sand   B. tar
   C. asbestos   D. high-temperature cement

22. The carbon dioxide (CO_2) content of the flue gases of an efficiently fired boiler should measure about

   A. 4%   B. 6%   C. 8%   D. 12%

23. Pre-heaters are generally installed when burning fuel oil number

   A. 6   B. 4   C. 2   D. 1

24. A typical boiler heat balance would show that the GREATEST amount of heat loss in boiler operation is

   A. in the slag   B. in the flue gases
   C. by radiation   D. by moisture in the air

25. When a boiler setting leaks air, there is an increase in the

   A. amount of heat lost
   B. boiler output
   C. quantity of flue gas impurities
   D. blow down

26. The 2 in a concrete mix of 1:2:4 refers to the quantity of

   A. cement   B. sand   C. water   D. filler

27. When roofing material is specified as *5 ply 70 lbs.*, it means that, as laid, the total of 5 plies weighs 70 lbs. per 100

   A. square feet   B. yards length
   C. square inches   D. feet length

28. The choice that shows which type of equipment is designed to prevent an elevator car from starting before the hatchway door is closed and locked is the

   A. hoistway access switch   B. interlocks
   C. spring buffer   D. counterweight

29. The piping through which water from private wells is delivered to swimming pools must be painted

    A. red   B. purple   C. orange   D. black

30. A chemical commonly used to disinfect swimming pools is

    A. ammonium nitrate   B. chloraseptic
    C. ammonium bicarbonate   D. calcium hypochorite

31. Shades and Venetian blinds are cleaned BEST with a

    A. dry cloth   B. scouring powder
    C. vacuum cleaner   D. paradry

32. The surfaces of water coolers and door kick plates are cleaned BEST by using a cleaning solution and a

    A. brush   B. wet cloth
    C. cellulose sponge   D. wad of paper

33. The BEST technique to use when washing the outside surface of the upper sash of double hung windows that are not equipped with safety belt anchors is to work from a

    A. standing position on the outside of the sill
    B. sitting position on the sill with the feet inside the room
    C. standing position on the inside of the sill
    D. standing position on the top of a stepladder

34. The one of the following that should be used to clean an acoustical ceiling is a

    A. dry mop   B. water wet cloth
    C. waxed cloth   D. vacuum cleaner

35. The BEST procedure to follow to determine the actual cleaning ability of a specific material is to

    A. test its performance
    B. read the specifications
    C. ask the manufacturer
    D. examine trade literature

36. The one of the following statements that is CORRECT concerning the application of wax by the use of a twine mop with handle is that

    A. infrequent heavy coats are preferred
    B. the mop used for waxing must be hard
    C. the wax should be poured from a pail onto the floor
    D. the wax should be applied in thin coats

37. One coat of floor sealer applied to a hardwood floor usually lasts

    A. at least 2 years   B. a maximum of 1 year
    C. no more than 6 months   D. no more than 3 months

38. The material recommended for removing blood or fruit stains from concrete is 38._____

   A. soft soap
   B. neatsfoot oil
   C. oxalic acid
   D. ammonia

39. To order wet mop filler replacements, you should specify the 39._____

   A. number of strands
   B. girth
   C. weight
   D. wet test strength

40. You should use chlordane in a building to control 40._____

   A. water seepage
   B. kitchen odors
   C. mildew
   D. roaches

KEY (CORRECT ANSWERS)

1.	D	11.	C	21.	C	31.	C
2.	A	12.	D	22.	D	32.	C
3.	B	13.	A	23.	A	33.	B
4.	C	14.	C	24.	B	34.	D
5.	D	15.	D	25.	A	35.	A
6.	C	16.	D	26.	B	36.	D
7.	C	17.	C	27.	A	37.	B
8.	C	18.	B	28.	B	38.	D
9.	C	19.	C	29.	A	39.	C
10.	B	20.	B	30.	D	40.	D

TEST 2

DIRECTIONS: Each question or incomplete statement is followed by several suggested answers or completions. Select the one that BEST answers the question or completes the statement. *PRINT THE LETTER OF THE CORRECT ANSWER IN THE SPACE AT THE RIGHT.*

1. Safety belts worn by window cleaners must meet the approval of the   1.____

   A. National Safety Council
   B. American Safety Council
   C. American National Standards Institute
   D. State Department of Labor

2. After a snowfall has stopped, all snow must be removed from sidewalks (the time between 9 P.M. and 7 A.M. excluded) within _____ hour(s).   2.____

   A. 4   B. 3   C. 2   D. 1

3. Little white insects that look like small shrimps and feed on the roots of grass are called   3.____

   A. grubs   B. ricks
   C. praying mantes   D. crabs

4. A term used to indicate a lawn chemical weed killer is   4.____

   A. germicide   B. emulsified
   C. herbicide   D. vitrified

5. A device installed in a drainage system to prevent gases from flowing into a building is called a   5.____

   A. trap   B. stall   C. cleanout   D. bidet

6. The plumbing fixture that contains a ball cock is the   6.____

   A. trap   B. water closet
   C. sprinkler   D. dishwasher

7. In a plumbing installation, an escutcheon is a   7.____

   A. metal collar   B. reducing tee
   C. valve   D. single sweep

8. A leaking faucet stem can be repaired by replacing the   8.____

   A. flange or the seat   B. nipple
   C. o-ring or the packing D. cock

9. The abbreviation *O.S. and Y.*, as used in plumbing, applies to a(n)   9.____

   A. hot well   B. radiator
   C. injector   D. gate valve

10. Gas range piping should have a minimum diameter of _____ inch.   10.____

    A. 3/4   B. 1/2   C. 1/4   D. 1/8

11. The pipe fitting that would be used to connect a 2" pipe at a 45-degree angle to another 2" pipe is called a(n)

    A. tee
    B. orifice flange
    C. reducer
    D. elbow

12. An instrument that measures relative humidity is called a(n)

    A. manometer
    B. interferometer
    C. hygrometer
    D. petrometer

13. The one of the following flat drive belts that gives the BEST service in dry places is a(n) _____ belt.

    A. rawhide
    B. oak-tanned
    C. chrome-tanned
    D. semirawhide

14. The letter representing the standard V-belt section which has the LOWEST horsepower-per-belt rating is

    A. E
    B. C
    C. B
    D. A

15. A 6 x 19 wire rope has

    A. 6 strands
    B. 6 wires in each strand
    C. 19 strands
    D. 25 strands arranged in a 6 x 19 pattern

16. A water tank that is 5 feet in diameter and 30 feet high has a volume of *most nearly* _____ cu.ft.

    A. 150
    B. 250
    C. 600
    D. 1200

17. The circumference of a circle with a radius of 5 inches is *most nearly* _____ in.

    A. 31.3
    B. 30.0
    C. 20.1
    D. 13.4

18. A flexible coupling should be used to connect two shafts that

    A. have centerlines at right angles to each other
    B. may be slightly out of line
    C. start and stop too fast
    D. have different speeds

19. Of the following materials used to make pipe, the one that is MOST brittle is

    A. lead
    B. aluminum
    C. copper
    D. cast iron

20. Mechanical equipment is generally tested and inspected on regular schedule in order to

    A. avoid breakdowns
    B. train new personnel
    C. maintain inventory
    D. give employees something to do

21. The *united inches* for a pane of glass that measures 14 inches by 20 inches is

   A. 14 B. 34 C. 40 D. 54

22. The one of the following that should NOT be lubricated is a(n)

   A. spur gear train
   B. motor commutator
   C. roller chain drive
   D. automobile axle

23. The one of the following oils that has the LOWEST viscosity is S.A.E.

   A. 70 B. 50 C. 20 D. 10W

24. A neoprene gasket would normally be used in a pipeline carrying

   A. steam
   B. compressed air
   C. carbon dioxide
   D. light oil

25. The one of the following that would NOT be used in cleaning toilet bowls is

   A. a cleaning cloth
   B. oxalic acid
   C. muriatic acid
   D. a detergent

26. An electric motor-driven air compressor is automatically started and stopped by a

   A. thermostat
   B. line air valve
   C. pressure switch
   D. float trap

27. The term *kilowatt hours* describes the consumption of

   A. energy
   B. radiation
   C. cooling capacity
   D. conductance

28. AC voltage may be converted to DC voltage by means of a

   A. magneto
   B. rectifier
   C. voltage regulator
   D. transducer

29. When replacing a blown fuse, it is BEST to

   A. install another one of slightly larger size
   B. seek the cause of the fuse failure before replacing it
   C. install another one of size smaller
   D. read the electric meters as a check on the condition of the circuit

30. A 208 volt, 3 phase, 4 wire circuit power supply has a line to grounded neutral voltage of approximately _____ volts.

   A. 120 B. 208 C. 220 D. 240

31. An interlock is generally installed on electronic equipment to

   A. prevent loss of power
   B. maintain vhf frequencies
   C. keep the vacuum tubes lit
   D. prevent electric shock during maintenance operations

32. A flame should NOT be used to inspect the electrolyte level in a lead acid battery because the battery cells give off highly flammable

    A. hydrogen
    B. lead oxide
    C. lithium
    D. xenon

33. The purpose of the third prong in a three-prong male electric plug used in a 120-volt circuit is to

    A. make a firm connection
    B. strengthen the plug
    C. prevent electric shock
    D. get more electricity

34. You are informed that an employee under your supervision has just been injured in the building. The FIRST course of action you should take is to

    A. inform your superior
    B. aid the injured employee
    C. call a meeting of all the men
    D. order an investigation

35. In the prevention of accidental injuries, the MOST effective procedure is to

    A. install safety guards
    B. alert the workers to the hazard
    C. install lighting for easy sight
    D. eliminate the accident hazard

36. The one of the following practices that will INCREASE the possibility of fires occurring is the

    A. using of understairs areas for storage of all kinds
    B. wiping of machinery shafts with lubricating oil
    C. ventilating of all storage spaces
    D. cleaning of lockers at frequent intervals

37. When evaluating a building for fire hazards, the MOST important considerations are the

    A. number of stories and the height of each story
    B. location in the neighborhood and the accessibility
    C. interior lighting and the furniture
    D. number of residents and the use of the building

38. The one of the following that is a basic safety requirement for operating a power mower is:

    A. Fill gasoline-driven mowers indoors
    B. Do not operate power mowers on wet grass
    C. Keep the motor running when you leave the mower unattended for only a short while
    D. Fill the tank while the engine is running

39. You observe a red truck making a fuel delivery. The fuel being delivered is probably

    A. gasoline
    B. #2 fuel oil
    C. #4 fuel oil
    D. #5 fuel oil

40. The one of the following steps that is NOT taken when operating a carbon dioxide fire extinguisher is to

    A. carry the extinguisher to the fire and set it on the ground
    B. unhook the hose
    C. pull the pin in the valve wheel
    D. turn the valve and direct the gas to the top of the fire

40.____

KEY (CORRECT ANSWERS)

1. D	11. D	21. B	31. D
2. B	12. C	22. B	32. A
3. A	13. B	23. D	33. C
4. C	14. D	24. D	34. B
5. A	15. A	25. C	35. D
6. B	16. C	26. C	36. A
7. A	17. A	27. A	37. D
8. C	18. B	28. B	38. B
9. D	19. D	29. B	39. A
10. A	20. A	30. A	40. D

EXAMINATION SECTION
TEST 1

DIRECTIONS: Each question or incomplete statement is followed by several suggested answers or completions. Select the one that BEST answers the question or completes the statement. *PRINT THE LETTER OF THE CORRECT ANSWER IN THE SPACE AT THE RIGHT.*

1. Of the following, the BEST way for you to make sure that a cleaner understands a spoken order which you have given to him is for you to

    A. ask him to repeat the order in his own words
    B. ask him whether he has understood the order
    C. watch how he begins to follow the order
    D. ask him whether he has any questions about the order

    1.____

2. You have called a meeting with your cleaners to get their suggestions on ways to keep up cleaning standards in spite of budget cutbacks.
You are MOST likely to be successful in encouraging them to participate in the discussion if you

    A. start the meeting by giving the cleaners all your own suggestions first
    B. keep the meeting going by talking whenever the cleaners have nothing to say
    C. get the cleaners to *think out loud* by asking them for their interpretations of the problem
    D. comment on and evaluate the suggestions made by each cleaner immediately after he makes them

    2.____

3. If a custodian knows that rumors being spread by his assistants are false, he should

    A. tell the assistants that the rumors are false
    B. tell the assistants the facts which the rumors have falsified
    C. threaten to discipline any assistant who spreads the rumors
    D. find out which assistant started the rumor and have him suspended

    3.____

4. One of your best cleaners tells you in private that he wants to quit his job.
The FIRST thing you should do in handling this matter is to

    A. ask the cleaner why he wants to quit his job
    B. tell the cleaner to take a few days to think it over
    C. refer the cleaner to the personnel office
    D. try to convince the cleaner not to quit his job

    4.____

5. The MOST important reason why a custodian should seek the suggestions of his cleaners on job-related matters is that the

    A. cleaners generally have greater knowledge of job-related matters than the custodian
    B. cleaners will tend to have a greater feeling of participation in their jobs by making suggestions
    C. custodian will be able to hold the cleaners responsible for any suggestions he follows
    D. custodian can win the respect of his cleaners by showing them the errors in their suggestions

    5.____

6. Your supervisor has ordered you to announce to your cleaners a new cleaning rule with which you disagree. You should

    A. admit honestly to your cleaners that you disagree with the rule
    B. announce the rule to your cleaners without expressing your disagreement
    C. encourage your cleaners by telling them you agree with the rule
    D. tell your supervisor that you refuse to announce any rule with which you disagree

7. Of the following, the BEST practice to follow in criticizing the work performance of a cleaner is to

    A. save up several criticisms and make them all at one time
    B. soften your criticisms by being humorous
    C. have another cleaner, who has more seniority, give the criticism
    D. make sure you explain to the cleaner the reasons for your criticism

8. The work goals which you set for your cleaners should be

    A. slightly less than their capabilities, so that they have some slack time
    B. approximately equal to their capabilities, so that they work at normal capacity
    C. slightly above their capabilities, so that they must extend themselves a little
    D. considerably above their capabilities, so that they must always be trying to catch up

9. Of the following, the BEST way to reduce unnecessary absences among your cleaners is to

    A. ask your cleaners the reason for their absence every time they are absent
    B. rely entirely on written warnings once every month to cleaners who have been absent too often during the month
    C. have your cleaners make a formal written report to you every time they are absent explaining the reason for their absence
    D. post publicly every month a list of those cleaners who you feel have been absent unnecessarily during the month

10. Of the following methods that might be used to deal with a cleaner who is habitually late for work without good reason, the BEST one for you to apply is to

    A. give the cleaner an assignment where his lateness will not inconvenience any other cleaner
    B. assign the cleaner to the most disagreeable jobs until he stops being late for work
    C. call the cleaner aside in private to give him a stern lecture on his habitual lateness
    D. appeal to the cleaner's better nature to urge him to correct his habitual lateness

11. To improve efficiency, you have instituted a new system of assigning work to your cleaners.
    Your cleaners are MOST likely to be cooperative in accepting this new system if you

    A. remind them how inefficient the former system was
    B. tell them of the advantages of the new system but not the disadvantages
    C. refuse to make any changes in the new system once you have instituted it
    D. follow-up on any problems the cleaners may have because of the new system

12. You are most likely to gain the wholehearted cooperation of your cleaners if you appeal MAINLY to their

    A. natural dislike for work
    B. fear of punishment
    C. satisfaction in a job well done
    D. desire to avoid responsibility

13. When combined with good leadership, regular inspections by a custodian of the work done by his cleaners can help create good morale MAINLY because the cleaners know that the custodian

    A. is interested in how they do their work
    B. will leave them alone between inspections
    C. may catch them if they do poor work
    D. does not rely on them to do their work unwatched

14. While you are making an inspection, you find two of your cleaners arguing angrily about the best procedure to follow in completing their assignment.
    Of the following, the FIRST thing you should do is to

    A. tell them that they will both be disciplined
    B. ignore the argument, since it is probably none of your business
    C. ask each one for his side of the argument
    D. order them to follow the procedure favored by the more experienced of the two

15. A one-person cleaning assignment which all of your cleaners find disagreeable comes up one day every month. It is BEST supervisory practice to assign

    A. each one in turn, by rotation
    B. anyone who happens to be available, by chance
    C. anyone you wish to punish for his poor work performance
    D. the one who is least likely to complain about the assignment

16. Despite your repeated warnings, one of your cleaners, through carelessness, has seriously damaged an expensive waxing machine.
    You are MOST likely to be effective in disciplining him if you

    A. reprimand him in the presence of the other cleaners
    B. consider his work record when deciding how to discipline him
    C. tell him that you will decide on a punishment for him during the following week
    D. make a point of reminding him frequently how he carelessly damaged an expensive waxing machine

17. A custodian is approached by a newspaper reporter and is asked questions about a certain member of the office staff. Of the following, the BEST course of action for the custodian to take is to

    A. ignore the newspaper reporter
    B. refer the newspaper reporter to the personnel office for information
    C. tell the newspaper reporter anything he wishes to know, but warn him that the information is not official
    D. give the newspaper reporter false information to discourage further questioning

18. While a custodian is making a note of the fluorescent lamps that need to be replaced in a waiting room, one of the waiting clients starts to complain angrily about the high cost of custodial services in the city.
    Of the following, the BEST course of action for the custodian to take is to

    A. tell the individual to be quiet and show more respect for city representatives
    B. try to persuade the person to take a more reasonable point of view
    C. listen courteously until the client has finished and then complain about the high cost of welfare
    D. ignore the comments and continue with his work

19. A group of workers complain to you about the lack of cleanliness in your building. You realize that budget cutbacks have unavoidably led to shortages in manpower and equipment for the cleaning staff.
    Of the following, the BEST way for you to answer these workers is to

    A. tell them frankly that the cleanliness of the building is none of their business
    B. apologize for the condition of the building and promise that your men will work harder
    C. tell them to take their complaints to the administration and not to you
    D. explain the reasons for the building's condition and what you are doing to improve it

20. The MOST important role of the custodian in promoting good public relations should be to help

    A. increase understanding between the custodial staff and the public which it serves
    B. keep from public attention any failings on the part of the custodial staff
    C. increase the authority of the custodial staff over the public with which it deals
    D. keep the public from interfering in the operations of the custodial staff

21. A supervisor conducting a staff meeting calls you to complain that the cleaners working in the empty office next to his are being unnecessarily noisy.
    Of the following, the BEST response to the supervisor is to tell him that

    A. he should go next door to tell the cleaners to stop the unnecessary noise
    B. you will tell the cleaners about his complaint and instruct them not to make unnecessary noise
    C. he should file a formal complaint against the cleaners with your superior
    D. you will come to his office to judge for yourself whether the cleaners are being unnecessarily noisy

22. The attitude a custodian should *generally* maintain toward the workers and office staff is one of

    A. avoidance   B. superiority
    C. courtesy   D. servility

23. A custodian notices that one of the clerks in using an unsafe electrical appliance which may cause a fire at any time.
Of the following, the BEST course of action for the custodian to take is to

   A. go into the clerk's office after hours and remove the appliance
   B. notify the fire department so that a summons will be served on the clerk
   C. go into the clerk's office after hours and damage the appliance in such a way as to eliminate the hazard
   D. speak to the clerk's supervisor privately and explain the danger and request that the supervisor ask the clerk to disconnect the appliance

24. An emergency has developed in which a custodian must enter a locked office to close some shut-off valves. The occupant of the office is a new employee who is alone and refuses to let the custodian in because she does not recognize him.
Of the following, the BEST course of action for the custodian to take is to

   A. force his way in and then apologize
   B. summon the police and explain that she is obstructing official city business
   C. show his credentials or seek out other individuals that the employee knows
   D. tell the employee that there is a fire in the building and her life is in danger

25. A telephone caller tells a building custodian that a bomb has been placed in the building and immediately hangs up the phone.
The FIRST thing the building custodian should do is to

   A. call the fire department
   B. call the police department
   C. let his subordinate handle it
   D. ignore the call, since most threats are hoaxes

KEY (CORRECT ANSWERS)

1. A
2. C
3. B
4. A
5. B
6. B
7. D
8. C
9. A
10. C

11. D
12. C
13. A
14. C
15. A
16. B
17. B
18. D
19. D
20. A

21. B
22. C
23. D
24. C
25. B

TEST 2

DIRECTIONS: Each question or incomplete statement is followed by several suggested answers or completions. Select the one that BEST answers the question or completes the statement. *PRINT THE LETTER OF THE CORRECT ANSWER IN THE SPACE AT THE RIGHT.*

1. Despite your repeated warnings, one of your custodial assistants, through carelessness, has seriously damaged an expensive paper shredder.
   You are MOST likely to be LEAST effective in disciplining him if you

   A. reprimand him in the presence of other custodial assistants
   B. consider his work record when deciding how to discipline him
   C. tell him that you will decide on a punishment for him during the following week
   D. make a point of reminding him now and then how he carelessly damaged an expensive paper shredder

2. Assume that one of your custodial assistants, although he does not drink on the job, is an alcoholic whose work performance has become inadequate because of his drinking problem.
   Of the following, the BEST approach to take in dealing with this custodial assistant is to

   A. do nothing, since he does not drink on the job
   B. recommend to your supervisor that the custodial assistant be fired because he is an alcoholic
   C. counsel him on the personal and emotional problems which cause his drinking problem
   D. advise him to seek professional help for his drinking problem

3. Of the following, you are MOST likely to be effective in training an inexperienced custodial assistant to do a complicated cleaning job if you

   A. train him in all parts of the job at the same time
   B. first demonstrate to him the most common errors in doing the job
   C. let him know from time to time how he is doing in learning the job
   D. encourage him in the beginning by overlooking any mistakes he may make

4. Praising a trainee who is making unusually good progress in learning from your training is *generally* considered to be

   A. *desirable*, because he is likely to be encouraged to continue making good progress
   B. *undesirable*, because he is likely to become overconfident and begin to do poorly
   C. *desirable*, because the other trainees are likely to become envious and try to compete with him
   D. *undesirable*, because he should not be praised for doing his job

5. Of the following, the MOST effective way for you to train a custodial assistant to perform a complicated cleaning job about which he has some knowledge is to

   A. let him do the entire job, then have him question you as to his problems
   B. repeat in your training what he already knows about the cleaning job
   C. teach him those parts of the job with which he is unfamiliar
   D. keep him slightly ill at ease during training

6. A custodial foreman in a large building should *normally* spend the GREATEST part of his working time on

   A. work planning
   B. records and reports
   C. personnel problems
   D. supervision and inspection

7. In general, the MOST efficient method for doing a cleaning job is the method which

   A. must be repeated most frequently
   B. has the most different steps and operations
   C. gives the best results for the least amount of effort
   D. requires the efforts of the greatest number of custodial assistants

8. If the directions given by your superior are not clear, the BEST thing for you to do is to

   A. ask to have the directions repeated and clarified
   B. proceed to do the work taking a chance on doing the right thing
   C. do nothing until some later time when you can find out exactly what is wanted
   D. ask one of the other men in your crew what he would do under the circumstances

9. Of the following procedures concerning grievances of subordinate personnel, the custodian-engineer should maintain an attitude of

   A. paying little attention to little grievances
   B. being very alert to grievances and make adjustments in existing conditions to appease all personnel
   C. knowing the most frequent causes of grievances and strive to prevent them from arising
   D. maintain rigid discipline of a nature that *smooths out* all grievances

10. Of the following, the BEST course of action to take to settle a dispute or conflict between two employees is to

    A. insist that the two employees settle the case between themselves
    B. call in each one separately and, after hearing their cases presented, decide the issue
    C. bring both in for a conference at the same time and make the decision in their presence
    D. have both present their points of view and arguments in written memoranda and on this basis make your decision

11. If, as a custodian-engineer, you discover an error in your report submitted to the main office, you should

    A. do nothing, since it is possible that one error will have little effect on the total report
    B. wait until the error is discovered in the main office and then offer to work overtime to correct it
    C. go directly to the supervisor in the main office after working hours and ask him unofficially to correct the error
    D. notify the main office immediately so that the error can be corrected, if necessary

12. There are a considerable number of forms and reports to be submitted on schedule by the custodian-engineer. The ADVISABLE method of accomplishing this duty is to

    A. fill out the reports at odd times during the days when you have free time
    B. schedule a definite period of the work-week for completing these forms and reports
    C. assign your foreman or cleaner to handle all these forms for you and to have them available on time
    D. classify or group the forms and reports and fill out only one of each group and refer the other forms or reports to the ones completed

13. A custodian-engineer can BEST evaluate the quality of work performed by custodial personnel by

    A. periodic inspection of the building's cleanliness
    B. studying the time records of personnel
    C. reviewing the building cleaning expenditures
    D. analyzing complaints of building occupants

14. Assume that you are the custodian-engineer and one of your employees wants to talk with you about a grievance. Of the following actions, the LEAST desirable action for you to take is to

    A. listen sympathetically
    B. conduct the discussion openly in the presence of the work-force
    C. try to get his point of view
    D. endeavor to obtain all the facts

15. Of the following factors, the one which is LEAST important in evaluating an employee and his work is his

    A. dependability   B. quantity of work
    C. quality of work   D. education and training

16. Supervision of a group of people engaged in building cleaning operations should NOT include supervision of

    A. time spent in cleaning operations
    B. utilization of official rest and lunch periods
    C. cleaning methods
    D. materials used for various cleaning jobs

17. Of the following methods, the BEST one to utilize in assigning custodial personnel to clean a multi-floor school building is to

    A. allow the cleaners to pick their rooms or area assignments out of a hat
    B. have the supervisor make specific room or area assignments to each cleaner separately
    C. rotate room and area assignments daily according to a chart posted on the bulletin board
    D. let a different member of the group make the room or area assignments each week

18. Assume that you are the custodian-engineer and that you have discovered a bottle of liquor in one of your employees' locker.
    The BEST course of action to take is to

A. fire him immediately
B. explain to him that liquor should not be brought into a school building and that a repetition may result in disciplinary action
C. suspend him until the end of the week and take him back only on a probational basis
D. assemble the staff and tell them they are all equally guilty for not having reported the matter to you

19. Of the following items, the one which is the LEAST important in the preparation of a report is that the report   19._____

   A. is brief, but to the point
   B. uses the prescribed form if there is one
   C. contains extra copies
   D. is accurate

20. In order to have building employees willing to follow standardized cleaning and maintenance procedures, the supervisor must be prepared to   20._____

   A. work alongside the employees
   B. demonstrate the reasonableness of the procedures
   C. offer incentive pay for their utilization
   D. allow the employees the free use of the time saved by their adoption

21. A fireman is frequently late in taking over his shift. In considering this situation, the factor which is of LEAST importance is   21._____

   A. the reason for his lateness
   B. how his lateness affects the work of other firemen
   C. how often he is late
   D. how willing he is to do emergency work

22. Suppose that you are preparing a requisition for cleaning supplies for the school year. The BEST single method of estimating the amount to be ordered is to   22._____

   A. ask each cleaner to submit an estimate of his needs for the coming year
   B. call other custodian-engineers to obtain from them an estimate of supply requirements
   C. confer with the school principal to obtain his estimate of school cleaning supply needs
   D. review the records of supplies used during the last few years

23. A number of injuries to pupils have occurred while they were traveling on the stairs of the school. Your inspection shows no defects or inadequacy of lighting.
The MOST desirable step to take to reduce the frequency of these accidents is to   23._____

   A. assign a cleaner to each stairway during the time the children use them
   B. put up signs warning the children to be careful
   C. suggest to the school principal that his teaching staff discuss the matter with the children
   D. install better lighting on the stairs and make certain that handrails are in perfect condition

24. The custodian-engineer, to be effective and efficient, must budget his time. This means MOST NEARLY that

   A. a value in dollars and costs should be placed on each hour's work of a custodian-engineer
   B. the custodian-engineer should make certain that all of his time, as well as that of his employees, is accounted for
   C. a time schedule for each employee must be prepared so that the yearly allowance for the school is not exceeded
   D. the custodian-engineer should plan his jobs and duties so that all can be covered as required

25. Suppose that a cleaner has been found to be quite negligent in his work and has been warned repeatedly by you.
   If you find that your warnings have not changed the man's attitude or work habits, the PROPER thing to do is to

   A. have the employee discharged
   B. change his assignment in the school to a less desirable job
   C. have a serious talk with the cleaner to find out why he does not do satisfactory work
   D. give the cleaner a final warning

KEY (CORRECT ANSWERS)

1. A
2. D
3. C
4. A
5. C

6. D
7. C
8. A
9. C
10. C

11. D
12. B
13. A
14. B
15. D

16. B
17. B
18. B
19. C
20. B

21. D
22. D
23. C
24. D
25. A

EXAMINATION SECTION
TEST 1

DIRECTIONS: Each question or incomplete statement is followed by several suggested answers or completions. Select the one that BEST answers the question or completes the statement. *PRINT THE LETTER OF THE CORRECT ANSWER IN THE SPACE AT THE RIGHT.*

1. Assume that a supervisor finds that his employees have become fatigued from doing a very long and repetitious job.
   The one of the following which would be the BEST way to relieve this fatigue is to
   A. assign other work so that the employees can switch to different assignments in the middle of the day
   B. let the employees listen to a radio while they work
   C. break the job down into very small parts so that each employee can concentrate on one simple task
   D. allow the employees to take frequent rest periods

   1.____

2. Assume that one of your subordinates is injured and will be out for at least six weeks.
   Of the following, the BEST way to handle the work normally assigned to this person is to
   A. allow the work to remain uncompleted until the injured person returns, since he is the one who can BEST do this work
   B. divide this work equally among the persons under your supervision who can do this work
   C. do all the work yourself
   D. give the injured person's work to the most efficient member of your staff

   2.____

3. Suppose that another supervisor tells you about a new way to organize some of your unit's work. The idea sounds good to you. However, before you were in this unit, a similar plan was tried and it failed.
   The MOST important thing for you to do FIRST is to
   A. find out why the previous attempt failed
   B. suggest that the other supervisor tell his idea to top management
   C. try the plan to see whether it works
   D. find proof that the plan has worked elsewhere

   3.____

4. One of your subordinates comes to you with a grievance. You discuss it with him so that you may fully understand the problem as he sees it. However, since you are uncertain as to the proper answer, you should
   A. tell him that you cannot help him with this problem
   B. tell him that you will have to check further and make an appointment to see him again
   C. send him to see your immediate superior for a solution to the problem
   D. ask him to find out from his co-workers whether this problem has come up before

   4.____

5. A supervisor reprimanded one of his subordinates severely for making a serious error in judgment while performing an assignment for which he had volunteered.
The supervisor's action was
   A. *incorrect*, chiefly because in the future the worker will probably try to avoid taking on responsibility
   B. *correct*, chiefly because this will insure that the worker will not make the same mistake in the future
   C. *correct*, chiefly because the worker should be discouraged from using his own judgment on the job
   D. *incorrect*, chiefly because the reprimand came too late to correct the error that had already been made

6. Of the following, the BEST way for a supervisor to inform all his subordinates of a change in lunch rules is, in MOST cases, to
   A. call a staff meeting
   B. tell each one individually
   C. issue a memorandum
   D. tell one or two employees to pass the word around

7. For a supervisor to assign work giving only general instructions to his subordinate would be advisable when
   A. the supervisor is confident that the worker knows how to do the job
   B. the assignment is a simple one
   C. the subordinate is himself a supervisory employee
   D. errors in the work will not cause serious delay

8. One of the DISADVANTAGES of setting minimum standards of performance for custodial employees is that
   A. such standards eliminate the basis for evaluating employees
   B. the custodial employees may keep their performance at the minimum level
   C. standards are always subject to change
   D. the supervisor may feel that his initiative is being restricted

9. One of your subordinates has been functioning below his usual level. You feel that something of a personal nature may be affecting his work. When you ask him casually whether anything is wrong, he says everything is fine.
As a next step, it would be BEST to
   A. make frequent casual and humorous comments about the poor quality of his work but refrain, at this time, from any serious discussion
   B. warn him that failure to maintain his customary level of performance might result in disciplinary action
   C. express your concern privately and reveal your interest in the reason for his change in work performance
   D. discuss with him the work of another employee, suggesting that the other employee would be a good example to follow

10. Assume you are teaching a new job to one of your subordinates. After you have demonstrated the job, you can BEST maintain the worker's interest by
    A. showing him training films about the job
    B. giving him printed material that explains why the job is important
    C. having him observe other workers do the job
    D. letting him attempt to do the job by himself under supervision

11. *Insubordination is sometimes a protest against inferior or arbitrary leadership.*
    For the supervisor, the MOST basic implication of the above statement is:
    A. Accusations of insubordination are easy to make, but usually difficult to prove.
    B. Insubordination cannot be permitted if an organization wishes to remain effective.
    C. When an employee discusses an order instead of carrying it out, he has not understood it.
    D. When an employee questions an order, review it to make sure it is reasonable.

12. In appraising a subordinate's mistakes, a supervisor should ALWAYS consider the
    A. absolute number of mistakes, without regard to severity
    B. number of mistakes in proportion to the number of decisions made
    C. total number of mistakes made by other, regardless of assignment
    D. number of mistakes which were discovered upon higher review

13. If you are the supervisor of an office in which the work frequently involves lifting heavy boxes, you should instruct your staff in the proper method of lifting to avoid injury.
    In giving these instructions, you should stress that a person lifting heavy objects MUST
    A. keep his feet close together
    B. bend at the waist
    C. keep his back as straight as possible
    D. use his back muscles to straighten up

14. Of the following, the BEST qualified supervisor is one who
    A. knows the basic principles and procedures of all the jobs which he supervises
    B. has detailed working knowledge of all aspects of the job he supervises but knows little about principles of supervision
    C. is able to do exceptionally well at least one of the jobs which he supervises and as some knowledge of the others
    D. knows little or nothing about most of the jobs which he supervises but knows the principles of supervision

15. The rate at which an employee will learn will vary according to a number of considerations.
    Of the following, which is LEAST likely to be controllable by the supervisor or the trainer? The
    A. manner in which the material is presented
    B. state of readiness of the learner
    C. scheduling of practice sessions
    D. nature of the material

16. When considering whether to use written material rather than oral instructions as a means of giving instructions to employees, the one of the following which should be given GREATEST consideration is the employees'
    A. personal preferences
    B. attitude toward supervision
    C. general educational level
    D. salary level

17. Assume that one of your subordinates has been assigned to attend job training classes.
    The one of the following which would probably be the BEST evidence of the success of the course is that the employee
    A. feels that he has learned something
    B. continues to study after the course is over
    C. has had a good class record
    D. improves in his work performance

18. Of the following, the situation LEAST likely to result if a supervisor shows favoritism toward particular employees is
    A. laxity in the work of the favored employees
    B. resentment from the other, less-favored employees
    C. increased ability among the favored employees
    D. lowering of morale among employees

19. The one of the following reasons for evaluating employees' performance, whether done formally or informally, which is NOT considered to be POSITIVE in nature is to
    A. give individual counsel to employees
    B. motivate employees toward improvement
    C. provide recognition of superior service
    D. set penalties for substandard performance

20. Assume that, because there has been an unexpected and temporary increase in the short-term work of your unit, you have had temporarily assigned to you several staff members from another agency.
    Of the following, in dealing with these employees, it would be LEAST advisable to
    A. assign them to long-term projects
    B. organize tasks so that they can begin work immediately
    C. set standards, making allowances to give them time to learn your ways
    D. direct them in the same way, in general, as you do your regular staff

21. It has been suggested that one way to increase employee productivity would be to require employees dealing with the public to have proficiency in a relevant foreign language.
Of the following, the MAJOR reason for implementing such a proposal, from the viewpoint of effective public administration, would be to
   A. encourage the foreign-born to learn English
   B. exchange information more rapidly and accurately
   C. increase the public prestige of the agency
   D. stimulate ethnic pride among all groups

21.____

22. Assume that the clerk who normally keeps your unit's records will be on vacation for four weeks.
If other clerks are equally qualified to keep these records, your BEST choice to replace the clerk would be the person who
   A. has skills which are needed least for other duties during this period
   B. volunteers for this work
   C. is next in turn for a special assignment
   D. has handled this task before

22.____

23. Assume that you have under your supervision several young clerical employees who have the bad habit of fooling around when they should be working.
Of the following, the BEST disciplinary action to take would be to
   A. ignore it; these young people will outgrow it
   B. join in the fun briefly in order to bring it to a quicker end each time it occurs
   C. bring to their attention the fact that this behavior is not acceptable and if it continues shift the make-up of the group to keep these young persons apart
   D. warn them that this type of behavior is reason for dismissal and be quick to make an example of the first one who starts it again

23.____

24. Seeking the advice of community leaders has human relations value for a public agency in planning or executing its programs CHIEFLY because it
   A. allows for the keeping of careful records concerning individual suggestions
   B. lets community leaders know that the agency has regard for their opinions
   C. permits the agency to state in writing which programs seem most appropriate
   D. unifies community leaders against the programs of competing private agencies

24.____

25. Good community relations is often action-oriented.
Which of the following activities of a public agency is LEAST likely to be considered as action-oriented by the people of a local community?
   A. Conducting a survey to gather information about the local community
   B. Extending the use of a facility to those previously excluded
   C. Providing a service that was formerly non-existent
   D. Removing something considered objectionable by the local community

25.____

KEY (CORRECT ANSWERS)

1. A
2. B
3. A
4. B
5. A

6. C
7. A
8. B
9. C
10. D

11. D
12. B
13. C
14. A
15. B

16. C
17. D
18. D
19. D
20. A

21. B
22. A
23. C
24. B
25. A

TEST 2

DIRECTIONS: Each question or incomplete statement is followed by several suggested answers or completions. Select the one that BEST answers the question or completes the statement. *PRINT THE LETTER OF THE CORRECT ANSWER IN THE SPACE AT THE RIGHT.*

1. Methods of communication with employees are of three types: oral, written, and visual.
   A MAJOR advantage of the written word is that it
   A. insures that content will remain unchanged no matter how many persons may be involved in its transmission
   B. facilitates two-way communication in delicate or confidential situations
   C. strengthens chain-of-command procedures in transmission of information and instruction by requiring the use of prescribed channels
   D. encourages the active participation of employees in the solution of complicated problems

   1.____

2. The use of the conference technique in training often requires more preparatory work on the part of the trainer than does a good lecture PRIMARILY because
   A. a conference would cover material of a more technical nature
   B. the trainer will be required to supply more printed material to the participants
   C. a conference usually involves a greater number of trainees
   D. the trainer must be prepared for a wide variety of possible occurrences

   2.____

3. The one of the following which is NOT an advantage of the lecture over most other methods of training is that it can be given
   A. over the radio or on record
   B. to large numbers of trainees
   C. without interruptions
   D. with little preparation

   3.____

4. Of the following, the one which is LEAST appropriate as a purpose for using an employee attitude survey is to
   A. develop a supervisory training program
   B. learn the identity of dissatisfied employees
   C. re-evaluate employee relations policies
   D. re-orient publications designed for employees

   4.____

5. The competent trainer seeks to become knowledgeable both in the work of the agency and in the duties of the positions for which he is to conduct training. Of the following, the GREATEST practical value that result when the trainer gains such knowledge is that
   A. he will be more likely to instruct employees to perform their work in a manner consistent with actual practice
   B. all levels of staff will be favorably impressed by a display of interest in the agency and its work
   C. employees will become familiar with the trainer and will not consider him an outsider
   D. the trainer will gain an accurate picture of the capacity of each employee for training

   5.____

6. Assume that you, the supervisor of a small office, are involved in planning the reorganization of your bureau's work. Management has decided not to inform your staff of the reorganization until the plans are completed.
   If one of your subordinates tells you that he has heard a rumor about reorganization of the department, you should reply that
   A. the reorganization involves the bureau, not the department
   B. you haven't heard anything about departmental reorganization and that he should stop spreading rumors
   C. you will inform your staff at the appropriate time if any definite plans are made involving a reorganization
   D. you do not know what is being planned but will ask your superior for details

7. Of the following training methods, the one in which the trainee's role is usually LEAST active is the _____ method.
   A. case-study
   B. conference
   C. group discussion
   D. lecture

8. Differences in morale between two work groups can sometimes be attributed to differences in the supervision they receive.
   Of the following, the behavior MOST characteristic of a supervisor of a group with high morale is that he
   A. assigns the least difficult tasks to employees with the most seniority
   B. is concerned primarily with his ultimate responsibility, production
   C. delegates authority and responsibility to his staff
   D. is lenient with his workers when they violate rules

9. Informal performance evaluations of individual employees, prepared systematically and regularly over a period of several years, are considered to be useful to a supervisor PRIMARILY because
   A. he will be able to assign tasks based only on these records
   B. unlike formal records, since they are fitted to the characteristics of individual employees, they provide for quick comparisons
   C. he need not discuss them with employees, since they are informal
   D. whatever personnel action he recommends can be substantiated by cumulative records

10. When instructing first-line supervisors in the proper method of evaluating the performance of probationary employees, it is LEAST important for a higher-level supervisor to
    A. explain in detail the standards to be used
    B. inform them of the possibility of higher management review
    C. caution them concerning common errors of evaluation
    D. mention the purposes of probationary employee evaluation

11. Assume that your agency is considering abolishing its official performance rating system but that you, a supervisor of a fairly large office, would like to devise a system for your own use.
    The FIRST step in setting up a system would be to
    A. decide what factors and personal characteristics are important and should be rated
    B. compare several rating methods to see which would be easiest to use
    C. have a private conference with each employee to discuss his performance
    D. set specific standards of employee performance, allowing your workers to make suggestions

11.____

12. The basic organizational structure of a municipal agency may have come about for several reasons.
    Of the following, the MOST important influence on the nature of its structure is the agency's
    A. professional attitude
    B. public reputation
    C. overall goal
    D. staff morale

12.____

13. The term *formal organization* refers to that organization structure agreed upon by top management whereas the term *informal organization* refers to the more spontaneous and flexible organizational ties developed by subordinates.
    The one of the following which BEST describes the usual *informal organization* is that it represents a(n)
    A. destructive system of relationships which should be eliminated
    B. concealed system of relationships whose goals are the same as management's
    C. actual system of relationships which should be recognized
    D. dysfunctional system of relationships which should be ignored

13.____

14. The reluctance of supervisors to delegate work to subordinates when they should is GENERALLY due to the supervisor's
    A. feelings of insecurity in work situations
    B. need to acquire additional experience
    C. inability to exercise control over his subordinates
    D. lack of technical knowledge

14.____

15. Assume that you have just been made the supervisor of a group of people you did not know before.
    For you to talk casually with each of your new subordinates with the purpose of getting to know them personally would be
    A. *advisable*, chiefly because subordinates have more confidence in a supervisor who shows personal interest in them
    B. *inadvisable*, chiefly because subordinates resent having their supervisor ask about their outside interests
    C. *advisable*, chiefly because one of the supervisor's main concerns should be to help his subordinates with their personal problems
    D. *inadvisable*, chiefly because a supervisor should not allow his relations with his subordinates to be influenced by their personalities

15.____

16. It has been found that high-producing subdivisions of organizations usually have supervisors whose behavior is employee-centered, whereas low-producing units usually have supervisors whose behavior is work-centered.
    Therefore, it could be concluded from these findings that
    A. a high-producing unit may cause a supervisor to be authoritarian
    B. a low-producing unit may cause a supervisor to be work-centered
    C. close supervision usually increases production
    D. employee-centered leadership may reduce production

17. A recent study in managerial science showed that, as the amount of praise increased and amount of criticism decreased, the supervisor was more likely to be perceived by his subordinates as being
    A. concerned with their career advancement
    B. production oriented, through subtle intimidation
    C. seeking personal satisfaction, irrespective of production
    D. uncertain of the subordinates' reliability

18. The power to issue directives or instructions to employees is derived from employees as much as from management.
    It follows MOST logically from this statement that
    A. attitudes toward management can be changed
    B. emphasis on discipline is needed
    C. authority is dependent upon acceptance
    D. employees should be properly supervised for work to be done

19. "In the decision-making process, it is a rare problem that has only one possible solution. Such a solution should be suspected of being nothing but a plausible argument for a preconceived idea."
    The author of the foregoing quotation apparently does NOT believe that
    A. there is usually only one possible solution to a problem
    B. the risks involved in any solution should be weighed against expected gains
    C. each alternative should be evaluated to determine the effort needed
    D. actions should be based on the urgency of problems

20. The supervisor who relies on punitive discipline to enforce his authority is putting limits on the potential of his leadership. Fear of punishment may secure obedience, but it destroys initiative. Such a supervisor's autocratic methods have cut off upward communications.
    Of the following, the major DISADVANTAGE of such autocratic behavior is that
    A. difficulties in the supervision of his subordinates will arise if limits are placed on the supervisor's responsibility
    B. policies that affect the public will be changed too frequently
    C. the supervisor will apply punishment subjectively rather than objectively
    D. instructions will be obeyed to the letter, regardless of changing circumstances

21. The need for a supervisor to carefully coordinate and direct the work of his unit increases as the work becomes 21.____
    A. more routine
    B. more specialized
    C. less complex
    D. less technical

22. The MAIN goal of discipline as used by a supervisor should be to 22.____
    A. keep the employees' respect
    B. influence behavior, so that work will be completed properly
    C. encourage the employees to work faster
    D. set an example for others

23. One of your subordinates has exhibited discourtesy and non-cooperation on several occasions. 23.____
    Of the following, the MOST appropriate attitude for you to adopt in dealing with this problem is that
    A. disciplinary measures for such an individual generally creates additional problems
    B. failure to correct such behavior may lead to worse offenses
    C. it is a mistake to make an issue out of minor infractions
    D. the harsher the medicine, the faster the cure

24. Assume that an employee has complained to you, his supervisor, that he cannot concentrate on his work because two of his co-workers make too much noise. You pay particular attention to these employees for several days and do not find them making excessive noise. 24.____
    The NEXT step you should take in handling this grievance is to
    A. have a talk with all three employees, urging them to cooperate and be considerate of one another
    B. arrange for the complainant to change his work location to a place away from the two co-workers
    C. talk to the complainant to find out if the complaint he made to you is the real cause of his dissatisfaction
    D. tell the complainant that you have found his grievance to be unfounded

25. In planning the application of an existing agency program to a local community, it is generally necessary to discover relevant problems and possibilities for service. 25.____
    Of the following, the BEST way to learn about such problems and possibilities for service would usually be to
    A. begin the program on a full-scale basis and await reactions
    B. seek opinions and advice from community residents and leaders
    C. hold staff meetings with agency employees who have worked in similar communities
    D. study official federal reports about already completed programs of the same kind

KEY (CORRECT ANSWERS)

1. A
2. D
3. D
4. B
5. A

6. C
7. D
8. C
9. D
10. B

11. A
12. C
13. C
14. A
15. A

16. B
17. A
18. C
19. A
20. D

21. B
22. B
23. B
24. C
25. B

TEST 3

DIRECTIONS: Each question or incomplete statement is followed by several suggested answers or completions. Select the one that BEST answers the question or completes the statement. *PRINT THE LETTER OF THE CORRECT ANSWER IN THE SPACE AT THE RIGHT.*

1. Which of the following characteristics would be LEAST detrimental to a supervisor in his efforts to set up and maintain good relations with other supervisors with whom he must deal in the course of his duties?
    A. Not getting involved in consultation on any supervisory problems they might have
    B. Indicating that they should improve their supervising methods and offering suggestions on how to do so
    C. Emphasizing his own role as a member of management
    D. Sharing information which has proved useful in his unit

    1.____

2. Both trainers and supervisors might agree that there is usually a best way to do a particular job. Yet a supervisor or instructor sometimes does not teach a new employee the best way, the most efficient way, to do a complex job.
    Sometimes, in such cases, the supervisor temporarily changes the sequence of operations, increases the number of steps needed to do a job, or makes other changes in the method, which then deviates from the one considered most efficient.
    When is such a difference in approach MOST justified when teaching a new employee a complex job?
    A. When the changes in approach correspond to the learning ability of the new employee
    B. When the new employee's performance on the job is closely supervised to compensate for a change in approach
    C. Where the steps in performing the task have not been defined in a manual of procedures
    D. When the instructor has ideas of improving upon the methods for doing the job

    2.____

3. Considerable thought in the field of management is directed toward the advantages and disadvantages of authoritarian methods of influencing behavior, and, in the so-called authoritarian model, a nucleus of rather consistent ideas prevail.
    Which of the following is LEAST characteristic of an administrative system based on the authoritarian model?
    A. A conviction of a need for order and efficiency in a world consisting mainly of people who lack direction and incentive
    B. Rules and contracts are the basis for action, and decisions are made on an impersonal basis
    C. The right to give orders and instructions is inherent in the hierarchical arrangement of an organizational structure
    D. Realization that subordinates' needs for affiliation and recognition can contribute to management's objectives

    3.____

4. Of the following, the FIRST step in planning an operation is to
   A. obtain relevant information
   B. identify the goal to be achieved
   C. consider possible alternatives
   D. make necessary assignments

5. A supervisor who is extremely busy performing routine tasks is MOST likely making incorrect use of what basis principle of supervision?
   A. Homogeneous Assignment
   B. Span of Control
   C. Work Distribution
   D. Delegation of Authority

6. Controls help supervisors to obtain information from which they can determine whether their staffs are achieving planned goals.
   Which one of the following would be LEAST useful as a control device?
   A. Employee diaries
   B. Organization charts
   C. Periodic inspections
   D. Progress charts

7. A certain employee has difficulty in effectively performing a particular portion of his routine assignments, but his overall productivity is average.
   As a direct supervisor of this individual, your BEST course of action would be to
   A. attempt to develop the investigator's capacity to execute the problematical facets of his assignments
   B. diversify the investigator's work assignments in order to build up his confidence
   C. reassign the investigator to less difficult tasks
   D. request in a private conversation that the investigator improve his work output

8. A supervisor who uses persuasion as a means of supervising a unit would GENERALLY also use which of the following practices to supervise his unit?
   A. Supervises and control the staff with an authoritative attitude to indicate that he is a *take-charge* individual
   B. Make significant changes in the organizational operations so as to improve job efficiency
   C. Remove major communication barriers between himself, subordinates, and management
   D. Supervise everyday operations while being mindful of the problems of his subordinates

9. Whenever a supervisor in charge of a unit delegates a routine task to a capable subordinate, he tells him exactly how to do it.
   This practice is GENERALLY
   A. *desirable*, chiefly because good supervisors should be aware of the traits of their subordinates and delegate responsibilities to them accordingly
   B. *undesirable*, chiefly because only non-routine tasks should be delegated
   C. *desirable*, chiefly because a supervisor should frequently test the willingness of his subordinates to perform ordinary tasks
   D. *undesirable*, chiefly because a capable subordinate should usually be allowed to exercise his own discretion in doing a routine job

10. The one of the following activities through which a supervisor BEST demonstrates leadership ability is by
    A. arranging periodic staff meetings in order to keep his subordinates informed about professional developments in the field of investigation
    B. frequently issuing definite orders and directives which will lessen the need for subordinates to make decisions in handling any investigations assigned to them
    C. devoting the major part of his time to supervising subordinates so as to stimulate continuous improvement
    D. setting aside time for self-development and research so as to improve the investigative techniques and procedures of his unit

11. The following three statements relate to supervision of employees:
    I. The assignment of difficult tasks that offer a challenge is more conducive to good morale than the assignment of easy tasks.
    II. The same general principles of supervision that apply to men are equally applicable to women.
    III. The best restraining program should cover all phases of an employee's work in a general manner.
    Which of the following choices lists ALL of the above statements that are generally CORRECT?
    A. II, III　　B. I　　C. I, II　　D. I, II, III

12. Which of the following examples BEST illustrates the application of the *exception principle* as a supervisory technique? A(n)
    A. complex job is divided among several employees who work simultaneously to complete the whole job in a shorter time
    B. employee is required to complete any task delegated to him to such an extent that nothing is left for the superior who delegated the task except to approve it
    C. superior delegates responsibility to a subordinate but retains authority to make the final decisions
    D. superior delegates all work possible to his subordinates and retains that which requires his personal attention or performance

13. Assume that you are a supervisor. Your immediate superior frequently gives orders to your subordinates without your knowledge.
    Of the following, the MOST direct and effective way for you to handle this problem is to
    A. tell your subordinates to take orders only from you
    B. submit a report to higher authority in which you cite specific instances
    C. discuss it with your immediate superior
    D. find out to what extent you authority and prestige as a supervisor have been affected

14. In an agency which has as its primary purpose the protection of the public against fraudulent business practices, which of the following would GENERALLY be considered an auxiliary or staff rather than a line function?

A. Interviewing victims of frauds and advising them about their legal remedies
B. Daily activities directed toward prevention of fraudulent business practices
C. Keeping records and statistics about business violations reported and corrected
D. Follow-up inspections by investigators after corrective action has been taken

15. A supervisor can MOST effectively reduce the spread of false rumors through the *grapevine* by
    A. identifying and disciplining any subordinate responsible for initiating such rumors
    B. keeping his subordinates informed as much as possible about matters affecting them
    C. denying false rumors which might tend to lower staff morale and productivity
    D. making sure confidential matters are kept secure from access by unauthorized employees

16. A supervisor has tried to learn about the background, education, and family relationships of his subordinates through observation, personal contact, and inspection of their personnel records.
    These supervisory actions are GENERALLY
    A. *inadvisable*, chiefly because they may lead to charges of favoritism
    B. *advisable*, chiefly because they may make him more popular with his subordinates
    C. *inadvisable*, chiefly because his efforts may be regarded as an invasion of privacy
    D. *advisable*, chiefly because the information may enable him to develop better understanding of each of his subordinates

17. In an emergency situation, when action must be taken immediately, it is BEST for the supervisor to give orders in the form of
    A. direct commands, which are brief and precise
    B. requests, so that his subordinate will not become alarmed
    C. suggestions, which offer alternative courses of action
    D. implied directive, so that his subordinates may use their judgment in carrying them out

18. When demonstrating a new and complex procedure to a group of subordinates, it is ESSENTIAL that a supervisor
    A. go slowly and repeat the steps involved at least once
    B. show the employees common errors and the consequences of such errors
    C. go through the process at the usual speed so that the employees can see the rate at which they should work
    D. distribute summaries of the procedure during the demonstration and instruct his subordinates to refer to them afterwards

19. The PRIMARY value of office reports and procedures is to
    A. assist top management in controlling key agency functions
    B. measure job performance
    C. save time and labor
    D. control the activities and use of time of all staff members

20. Of the following, which is considered to be the GREATEST advantage of the oral report? It
    A. allows for accurate transmission of information from one individual to another
    B. presents an opportunity to discuss or clarify any immediate questions raised by the receiver of the report
    C. requires less office work to maintain records on actions taken when an oral report is involved
    D. takes only a short amount of time to plan and prepare material for an oral report

21. A supervisor who is to make a report about a job he has done can make an oral report of a written report.
    Of the following, which is the BEST time to make an oral report? When
    A. the work covers an emergency situation
    B. a record is needed for the files
    C. the report is channeled to other departments
    D. the report covers additional work he will do

22. Suppose that a new employee has been assigned to you. It is your responsibility to see to it that he understands how to fill out properly the forms he is required to use.
    What would be the BEST way to do this?
    A. Explain the use of each form to the new technician and show him how to fill them out
    B. Give the new employee a copy of each form he must use so that he can learn by studying them
    C. Ask an experienced worker to explain clearly to him how the forms should be filled out
    D. Tell the new employee that filling out forms is simple and he should follow the instructions on each form

23. As a supervisor, you want to have your staff take part in improving work methods.
    Of the following, the BEST way to do this is to
    A. make critical appraisals of their work frequently
    B. encourage them to make suggestions
    C. make no change without their approval
    D. hold regular staff meetings

24. A good relationship with other supervisors is important to a senior supervisor. Close cooperation among supervisory personnel is MOST likely to result in
    A. increasing the probability for support of supervisory actions and decisions
    B. stimulating supervisors to achieve higher status in the organization
    C. helping to control the flow of work within a unit
    D. a clearer definition of the responsibilities of individual supervisors

25. Which of the following is MOST likely to gain a supervisor the respect and cooperation of his staff?
    A. Assigning the most difficult jobs to the experienced staff members
    B. Giving each staff member the same number of assignments
    C. Assigning jobs according to each staff member's ability
    D. Giving each staff member the same types of assignments

KEY (CORRECT ANSWERS)

1.	D	11.	C
2.	A	12.	D
3.	D	13.	C
4.	B	14.	C
5.	D	15.	B
6.	B	16.	D
7.	A	17.	A
8.	D	18.	A
9.	D	19.	A
10.	C	20.	B

21. A
22. A
23. B
24. A
25. C

READING COMPREHENSION
UNDERSTANDING AND INTERPRETING WRITTEN MATERIAL
EXAMINATION SECTION
TEST 1

Questions 1-10.

DIRECTIONS: Each question or incomplete statement is followed by several suggested answers or completions. Select the one that BEST answers the question or completes the statement. *PRINT THE LETTER OF THE CORRECT ANSWER IN THE SPACE AT THE RIGHT.*

1. Accident prevention is an activity which depends for success upon factual information, research, and analysis. Experience has proved that all accidents can be prevented through the correct application of basic accident prevention methods and techniques determined from factual cause data. Therefore, to achieve the maximum results from any safety and health program, a uniform system for the reporting of accidents and causes is established. The procedures required for a report, when properly carried out, will determine accurate cause factors and the most practical methods for applying preventive or remedial action. According to the above paragraphs, which of the following statements is MOST NEARLY correct? 1._____

   A. No matter how much effort is put forth, there are some accidents that cannot be prevented.
   B. Accident prevention is a research activity.
   C. Accident reporting systems are not related to accident prevention.
   D. The success of an accident prevention program depends on the correct use of a uniform accident reporting system.

Questions 2-7.

DIRECTIONS: Questions 2 through 7 are to be answered ONLY according to the information given in the following accident report.

DATE: February 2

TO: Edward Moss, Superintendent
Pacific Houses
2487 Shell Road
Auburnsville, Illinois

SUBJECT: Report of Accident to
Philip Fay, Employee
1825 North 8th St.
Auburnsville, Ill.
Identification #374-24

Philip Fay, an employee, came to my office at 10:15 A.M. yesterday and told me that he hurt his left elbow. When I asked him what happened, he told me that 15 minutes ago, while shoveling the snow from in front of Building #14 at 2280 Stone Ave., he slipped on some snow-covered ice and fell on his elbow. Joseph Sanchez and Arthur Campbell, who were working with him, saw what happened.

105

Mr. Fay complained of pain and could not bend his left arm. I called for an ambulance right away. A police patrol car from the 85th Precinct arrived 15 minutes later, and Patrolman Johnson, Shield #8743, said that an ambulance was on the way. At 10:45 A.M., an ambulance arrived from Auburn Hospital. Dr. Breen examined Mr. Fay and told me that he would have to go to the hospital for some x-ray pictures to determine how bad the injury was. The ambulance left with Mr. Fay at 11:00 A.M.

At 3:45 P.M., Mr. Fay called from the hospital and told me that his arm had been put in a cast in the emergency room of the hospital. He was told that he had fractured his left elbow and would have to stay out of work for about four weeks. He is to report back at the hospital in three weeks for another examination and to see if the cast can be taken off. His wife was at the hospital with him, and they were now going home.

Attached are the statements from the witnesses and our completed REPORT OF INJURY form.

                                William Fields
                                Foreman

2. Which one of the following did NOT see the accident?

   A. Campbell   B. Fay   C. Fields   D. Sanchez

3. The CORRECT date and time of accident is February

   A. 2, 10:00 A.M.   B. 2, 10:15 A.M.
   C. 1, 10:00 A.M.   D. 1, 10:15 A.M.

4. The ambulance came about _____ hour after _____.

   A. 1/4 ; the accident   B. 1/4 ; it was called
   C. 1/2; the accident   D. 1/2; it was called

5. It is not possible to tell whether Fay went to report the accident right away because the report does NOT say

   A. how long it takes to get from Building #14 to the foreman's office
   B. how long it takes to get from Stone Ave. to Shell Rd.
   C. whether Fay telephoned the foreman first
   D. whether the foreman was in his office as soon as Fay got there

6. From the facts in the report, Fay's action might be criticized because he

   A. did not give the foreman the complete story of what had happened
   B. did not take Campbell or Sanchez with him when he went to the foreman's office in case he should need help on the way
   C. did not remain at the accident site and send Sanchez and Campbell to bring the foreman
   D. telephoned from the hospital and by using his arm to do this he might have aggravated his condition

7. Assuming that the report gives the complete story of this incident, the action of the foreman may be criticized because he did NOT

   A. call an ambulance soon enough
   B. go to the hospital with the ambulance and stay with the injured man until he was discharged
   C. have the injured man sign a release of claim against the department
   D. make an on-the-spot investigation of the accident scene nor take corrective action

Questions 8-10.

DIRECTIONS: Questions 8 through 10 are to be answered ONLY according to the information given in the following passage.

A foreman has four maintainers and two helpers assigned to him. Listed below are the maintainers and helpers and their rate of speed in completing the assignments given to them. Assume all the foreman's men (maintainers and helpers) are of equal technical ability but some work faster than others while some are slower in completing their assignments. In all cases, no overtime is to be granted.

   Maintainer E - works at average rate of speed
   Maintainer F - works at twice the rate of speed as Maintainer E
   Maintainer G - works at the same rate of speed as Maintainer E
   Maintainer H - works at half the rate of speed as Maintainer E
   Helper J - works at same rate of speed as Maintainer G
   Helper K - works at same rate of speed as Maintainer H

8. A certain job must be done immediately, and Maintainer H and Helper J are the only men available.
   If Maintainer F, working alone, could normally complete this job in six days, the TOTAL time this foreman should allot to Maintainer H and Helper J to complete the same job is _____ days.

   A. 3   B. 4   C. 8   D. 12

9. While Maintainer E and Helper J are working on a job, Helper J reports that he will be out sick for at least a week. The job normally would have taken four more days to complete, and it must be completed within these four days.
   If Maintainer H and Helper K are the only two men available, this foreman should

   A. assign Helper K to replace Helper J
   B. assign Maintainer H to replace Helper J
   C. assign both Maintainer H and Helper K to replace Helper J
   D. inform his assistant supervisor that the job cannot be completed on time

10. This foreman has assigned all six of his men to a routine maintenance job. At the end of two days, the job is four-fifths completed; and instead of reassigning all his men the following day when they would finish early, the foreman cuts the gang so that the job will take one more full day to finish. The work gang on the last day should consist of Maintainer(s)

    A. F and H   B. F and Helper J
    C. E and Helpers J and K   D. G and H and Helper K

Questions 11-25.

DIRECTIONS: Each question consists of a statement. You are to indicate whether the statement is TRUE (T) or FALSE (F). *PRINT THE LETTER OF THE CORRECT ANSWER IN THE SPACE AT THE RIGHT.*

Questions 11-15.

DIRECTIONS: Questions 11 through 15 are to be answered ONLY according to the information given in the following paragraph.

USING LADDERS

All ladders must be checked each day for any defects before they are used. They should not be used if there are split rails or loose rungs or if they have become shaky. Two men should handle a stepladder which is over eight feet in height, one man if the ladder is smaller. One man must face the ladder and hold it with a firm grasp while the other is working on it. When you climb a ladder, always face it, grasp the siderails, and climb up one rung at a time. You should come down the same way.

11. A ladder which is new does not have to be inspected before it is used. 11.____

12. A ladder with a loose rung may be used if this rung is not stepped on. 12.____

13. A stepladder 6 feet long may be handled by one man. 13.____

14. If a 10-foot stepladder is used, one man must hold the ladder while the other works on it. 14.____

15. The siderails of a ladder do not have to be held when climbing down. 15.____

Questions 16-20.

DIRECTIONS: Questions 16 through 20 are to be answered ONLY according to the information given in the following paragraph.

TRAFFIC ACCIDENTS

Three auto accidents happened at the corner of Fifth Street and Seventh Avenue. The first, at 7:00 P.M. last night, knocked down a light pole when two cars collided. At 8:15 A.M. this morning, two other autos crashed head on. This afternoon, at 12:30 P.M., another pair of cars crashed. One of them jumped the curb, knocked over two traffic signs, and damaged three parked cars at the corner service station. No serious injury to the drivers was reported, but all the cars involved were severely damaged.

16. Nine cars were damaged in the three accidents. 16.____

17. The three accidents happened within a period of 14 hours. 17.____

18. A service station is located at the corner of Fifth Street and Seventh Avenue. 18.____

19. In the last accident, both cars jumped the curb and knocked over two light poles. 19.____

20. The drivers of the cars in the last accident were badly hurt. 20.____

Questions 21-25.

DIRECTIONS: Questions 21 through 25 are to be answered ONLY according to the information given in the following paragraph.

LIFTING

Improper lifting of heavy objects is a frequent cause of strains and ruptures. When a heavy object is to be lifted, an employee should stand close to the object and face it squarely. The feet are spread slightly apart, and one foot is a little ahead of the other. Then, bend the knees to bring the body down to the object and keep your back comfortably vertical. Raise the object slightly to see if you can lift it alone. If you can, get a firm grasp with both hands, balance the object, and raise it by straightening the legs, but still keeping the back erect. The raising motion is gradual, not swift. In this way you use the leg muscles which are the strongest muscles in the body. This method of lifting prevents strain to the back muscles which are weak and not built for lifting purposes.

21. Many ruptures are the result of not lifting heavy objects in the correct manner.   21.____

22. When an employee lifts a heavy package, he should keep his feet close together in order to balance the load.   22.____

23. When lifting a heavy object, the back should not be bent but kept upright.   23.____

24. It is best to lift heavy objects quickly in order to prevent strains and ruptures.   24.____

25. For purposes of lifting, the leg muscles are stronger than the arm muscles.   25.____

KEY (CORRECT ANSWERS)

1.	D	11.	F
2.	C	12.	F
3.	C	13.	T
4.	D	14.	T
5.	A	15.	F
6.	B	16.	T
7.	D	17.	F
8.	C	18.	T
9.	C	19.	F
10.	B	20.	F

21. T
22. F
23. T
24. F
25. T

TEST 2

DIRECTIONS: Each question or incomplete statement is followed by several suggested answers or completions. Select the one that BEST answers the question or completes the statement. *PRINT THE LETTER OF THE CORRECT ANSWER IN THE SPACE AT THE RIGHT.*

Questions 1-8.

DIRECTIONS: Questions 1 through 8, inclusive, are based on the ladder safety rules given below. Read these rules fully before answering these questions.

LADDER SAFETY RULES

When a ladder is placed on a slightly uneven supporting surface, use a flat piece of board or small wedge to even up the ladder feet. To secure the proper angle for resting a ladder, it should be placed so that the distance from the base of the ladder to the supporting wall is one-quarter the length of the ladder. To avoid overloading a ladder, only one person should work on a ladder at a time. Do not place a ladder in front of a door. When the top rung of a ladder rests against a pole, the ladder should be lashed securely. Clear loose stones or debris from the ground around the base of a ladder before climbing. While on a ladder, do not attempt to lean so that any part of the body, except arms or hands, extends more than 12 inches beyond the side rail. Always face the ladder when ascending or descending. When carrying ladders through buildings, watch for ceiling globes and lighting fixtures. Avoid the use of rolling ladders as scaffold supports.

1. A small wedge is used to

   A. even up the feet of a ladder resting on an uneven surface
   B. lock the wheels of a roller ladder
   C. secure the proper resting angle for a ladder
   D. secure a ladder against a pole

2. An 8-foot ladder resting against a wall should be so inclined that the distance between the base of the ladder and the wall is _____ feet.

   A. 2   B. 5   C. 7   D. 9

3. A ladder should be lashed securely when

   A. it is placed in front of a door
   B. loose stones are on the ground near the base of the ladder
   C. the top rung rests against a pole
   D. two people are working from the same ladder

4. Rolling ladders

   A. should be used for scaffold supports
   B. should not be used for scaffold supports
   C. are useful on uneven ground
   D. should be used against a pole

5. When carrying a ladder through a building, it is necessary to

   A. have two men to carry it
   B. carry the ladder vertically
   C. watch for ceiling globes
   D. face the ladder while carrying it

6. It is POOR practice to

   A. lash a ladder securely at any time
   B. clear debris from the base of a ladder before climbing
   C. even up the feet of a ladder resting on slightly uneven ground
   D. place a ladder in front of a door

7. A person on a ladder should NOT extend his head beyond the side rail by more than _____ inches.

   A. 12   B. 9   C. 7   D. 5

8. The MOST important reason for permitting only one person to work on a ladder at a time is that

   A. both could not face the ladder at one time
   B. the ladder will be overloaded
   C. time would be lost going up and down the ladder
   D. they would obstruct each other

Questions 9-13.

DIRECTIONS: Questions 9 through 13 concern an excerpt of written material which you are to read and study carefully. The excerpt is immediately followed by five statements which refer to it alone. You are required to judge whether each statement

   A. is entirely true
   B. is entirely false
   C. is partly true and partly false
   D. may or may not be true but cannot be answered on the basis of the facts as given in the excerpt

It is true that in 1987 there were more strikes than in any year, excepting 1986, since 1970. However, the number of workers involved was less in 1987 than in any year since 1981, and man-days of idleness due to strikes, the MOST accurate measure of industrial strife, were less in 1987 than in any year since 1980, again excepting 1986.

9. There were fewer workers involved in strikes in 1986 than in 1981.

10. There were more strikes in 1986 than in 1987.

11. There were more strikes in 1986 than in 1970.

12. There were fewer workers involved in strikes but more man-days of idleness in 1981 than 1987.

13. There were fewer man-days of idleness and fewer workers involved in strikes in 1986 than 1987.

13._____

Questions 14-16.

DIRECTIONS: Questions 14 through 16 are to be answered on the basis of the information given in the following passage.

Telephone service in a government agency should be adequate and complete with respect to information given or action taken. It must be remembered that telephone contacts should receive special consideration since the caller cannot see the operator. People like to feel that they are receiving personal attention and that their requests or criticisms are receiving individual rather than routine consideration. All this contributes to what has come to be known as Tone of Service. The aim is to use standards which are clearly very good or superior. The factors to be considered in determining what makes good Tone of Service are speech, courtesy, understanding, and explanations. A caller's impression of Tone of Service will affect the general attitude toward the agency and city services in general.

14. The above passage states that people who telephone a government agency like to feel that they are

14._____

   A. creating a positive image of themselves
   B. being given routine consideration
   C. receiving individual attention
   D. setting standards for telephone service

15. Which of the following is NOT mentioned in the above passage as a factor in determining good Tone of Service?

15._____

   A. Courtesy   B. Education
   C. Speech   D. Understanding

16. The above passage IMPLIES that failure to properly handle telephone calls is *most likely* to result in

16._____

   A. a poor impression of city agencies by the public
   B. a deterioration of courtesy toward operators
   C. an effort by operators to improve the Tone of Service
   D. special consideration by the public of operator difficulties

Questions 17-20.

DIRECTIONS: Questions 17 through 20 are to be answered ONLY according to the information given in the following passage.

ACCIDENT PREVENTION

Many accidents and injuries can be prevented if employees learn to be more careful. The wearing of shoes with thin or badly worn soles or open toes can easily lead to foot injuries from tacks, nails, and chair and desk legs. Loose or torn clothing should not be worn near moving machinery. This is especially true of neckties which can very easily become caught in the machine. You should not place objects so that they block or partly block hallways, corridors, or other passageways. Even when they are stored in the proper place, tools, supplies, and equipment should be carefully placed or piled so as not to fall, nor have anything stick out from a pile. Before cabinets, lockers or ladders are moved, the tops should be cleared of anything which might injure someone or fall off. If necessary, use a dolly to move these or other bulky objects.

Despite all efforts to avoid accidents and injuries, however, some will happen. If an employee is injured, no matter how small the injury, he should report it to his supervisor and have the injury treated. A small cut that is not attended to can easily become infected and can cause more trouble than some injuries which at first seem more serious. It never pays to take chances.

17. According to the above passage, the one statement that is NOT true is that 17.____

    A. by being more careful, employees can reduce the number of accidents that happen
    B. women should wear shoes with open toes for comfort when working
    C. supplies should be piled so that nothing is sticking out from the pile
    D. if an employee sprains his wrist at work, he should tell his supervisor about it

18. According to the above passage, you should NOT wear loose clothing when you are 18.____

    A. in a corridor   B. storing tools
    C. opening cabinets   D. near moving machinery

19. According to the above passage, before moving a ladder you should 19.____

    A. test all the rungs
    B. get a dolly to carry the ladder at all times
    C. remove everything from the top of the ladder which might fall off
    D. remove your necktie

20. According to the above passage, an employee who gets a slight cut should 20.____

    A. have it treated to help prevent infection
    B. know that a slight cut becomes more easily infected than a big cut
    C. pay no attention to it as it can't become serious
    D. realize that it is more serious than any other type of injury

Questions 21-24.

DIRECTIONS: Questions 21 through 24 are to be answered on the basis of the following report.

TO: Thomas Smith   Date: June 14.
        Supervising Menagerie Keeper
                                                Subject:
FROM: Jay Jones
        Senior Menagerie Keeper

On June 14, a visitor to the monkey house at the zoo was noticed annoying the animals. He was frightening the animals by making loud noises and throwing stones at the animals in the cages. The visitor was asked to stop annoying the animals but did not. And he was then asked to leave the monkey house by the keeper on duty. The visitor would not leave and said that the zoo is public property and that as a citizen he has every right to be there. The keeper kept trying to pursuade the visitor to leave but was unsuccessful. The keeper finally threatened to call the police. The visitor soon left the monkey house and did not return. Fortunately, no animals were harmed in this incident.

21. The subject of the report has been left out.
    Which one of these would be the BEST statement for the subject of the report?

    A. Loud noises in the monkey house
    B. Police called to monkey house
    C. Visitor annoying monkeys on June 14
    D. Monkeys unharmed by visitor

22. Which one of these is an important piece of information that should have been included in the FIRST sentence of the report?

    A. The kinds of monkeys in the monkey house
    B. Whether the visitor was a man or a woman
    C. The address of the monkey house
    D. The name of the zoo where the incident took place

23. The fourth sentence which begins with the words *And he was then asked...* is poorly written because

    A. the sentence begins with *And*
    B. the words *monkey house* should be written *Monkey House*
    C. the words *on duty* should be written *on-duty*
    D. *didn't* would be better than *did not*

24. In the sixth sentence, which begins with the words *The keeper kept trying...* , a word that is spelled wrong is

    A. trying   B. pursuade
    C. visitor   D. unsuccessful

Questions 25-27.

DIRECTIONS: Questions 25 through 27 test how well you can read and understand what you read. Read about ELEPHANTS. Then, on the basis of what you read, answer these questions.

ELEPHANTS

Elephants are peaceful animals and have very few real natural enemies. As with many other animals, when faced with danger the elephant tries to make himself look larger to his enemy. He does this by raising his head and trunk to look taller. The elephant will also extend his ears to look wider. Other threatening gestures may be made. The elephant may shift his weight from side to side, make a shrill scream, or pretend to charge with his trunk held high. If the enemy still fails to retreat, the elephant will make a serious attack.

25. When an elephant is in danger, he tries to make it appear that he is

    A. stronger   B. smaller   C. larger   D. angry

26. When he is threatened, an elephant tries to make himself look broader by   26._____

    A. taking a deep breath
    B. spreading out his ears
    C. shifting his weight from side to side
    D. holding his trunk high

27. If his enemy does not run away, the elephant will   27._____

    A. attack him
    B. run in the opposite direction
    C. hit the enemy with his trunk
    D. make a shrill scream

Questions 28-30.

DIRECTIONS: Read about PREVENTING DISEASE. Then, on the basis of what you read, answer Questions 28 through 30.

PREVENTING DISEASE

Proper feeding, housing, and handling are important in maintaining an animal's defenses against disease and parasites. The best diets are those that contain proteins, vitamins, minerals, and the other essential food elements. Proteins are especially important because they are necessary for growth. Minerals such as iron, copper, and cobalt help correct anemia. It has been shown that an animal's resistance can be decreased by improper feeding. However, it has not been proved that the use of certain types of feeds will increase the resistance of animals to infectious diseases. If animals are kept in good condition by proper diet and sanitary conditions, natural resistance to disease and parasites will be highest.

28. Food elements that are required especially for growth are   28._____

    A. minerals   B. vitamins
    C. proteins   D. carbohydrates

29. If animals are NOT fed correctly, they will   29._____

    A. have more diseases
    B. fight with each other
    C. need more proteins
    D. be able to kill parasites

30. The bodies of animals will BEST be able to fight disease naturally when they   30._____

    A. are kept warm
    B. are given immunity shots
    C. are given extra food
    D. have good diet and clean quarters

KEY (CORRECT ANSWERS)

1.	A	16.	A
2.	A	17.	B
3.	C	18.	D
4.	B	19.	C
5.	C	20.	A
6.	D	21.	C
7.	A	22.	D
8.	B	23.	A
9.	B	24.	B
10.	A	25.	C
11.	D	26.	B
12.	A	27.	A
13.	C	28.	C
14.	C	29.	A
15.	B	30.	D

HVAC TERMS

Basic Cooling Circuit
Basic cooling is heat-moving - heat absorption. Heat is absorbed when liquid is boiled to a vapor. The temperature at which liquid boils is determined by pressure. Reducing pressure lowers the boiling point, and increasing pressure raises the boiling point. Water boils at 212°F at sea level; higher altitude lowers the boiling point. Boilers use the principle of heating water under pressure to raise the boiling point.

Simple Cooling Circuit = enclosed chamber (evaporator), compressor, expansion device, metering device, discharge device, filter-drier sight glass

Compressor
Maintains low pressure - reduces pressure on vapor on intake stroke, compresses vapor on compression stroke, discharges vapor under high pressure at outlet.

Compressors = Reciprocating piston driven by internally sealed motor or shaft driven by external (open-drive) motor. Hermetically sealed/welded housing; semi-hermetically bolted housing. Seal on the open drive is a disadvantage; it may leak. Small appliance compressors are often the rotary type, hermetically sealed. Residential A/C, refrigeration, hermetic/semi-hermetic rec. piston or scroll type. Large compressors (chillers, cooling plants) rec./screw/centrifugal type. Must cool compressor motor.

Expansion Device = expansion valve, capillary tube, fixed restrictor. Small, easily clogged orifices.

Low Side = metering device, evaporator, expansion device, and intake (suction) side of compressor. Accumulator traps liquid at outlet of evaporator. Low side pressures are typically under 100 psi.

High Side = discharge side of compressor, condenser and liquid line. Receivers to store excess refrigerant at outlet of condenser.

Filter-Drier
Filters contaminants, removes moisture. Sight glass in liquid line to view flow. Indicator of proper charge is solid liquid flowing through sight glass.

Condenser
High pressure heat transfer coil; accepts high temperature-high pressure gas from compressor, cools and condenses it to a low temperature-high pressure liquid.

Refrigerant
Liquid with a boiling point below desired evaporator temperature. For A/C refrigerants a boiling point below 70° F.

Access = pinched-off tubes (small), Schrader valves (medium), service valves (large, 3 positions)

Relief valves = protect against excessive high pressure. Relief valves cannot be installed in series. Test pressures cannot exceed rating on dataplate.

Superheated gas ideal for compressors (no liquid).

Compressor Lubricants
Long list of requirements. High miscibility (ability to mix with refrigerants). Polyester or "ester" based lubricants. Use alkylbenzenes for ternary blends containing HCFC's. Generally never mix lubricants.

Leak Detection
System must be sealed for reliability and environment.

Vacuum Pump
System must be evacuated and dehydrated prior to charging. Contaminants change pressure/temperature relationship and will cause system failure. Acids produced will corrode metal parts, decrease performance, and increase service needs.

Evacuation Procedure
Pressure Readings = relative to a pressure zone.
Absolute Pressure = outer space, total vacuum, zero pressure (0 psi Absolute)
Gauge Pressure = pressure relative to atmospheric pressure of 14.7 psi.
A gauge calibrated to read absolute pressure reads 14.7 *psia*. When disconnected at sea level, it reads 0 psia in deep space. A gauge calibrated to read gauge pressure reads 0 *psig* when disconnected at sea level and -14.7 psig in space. Gauge readings are more useful in A/C-Refrigeration. Temperature/pressure charts generally use gauge and Fahrenheit values.
Inches of Mercury (in Hg) are used for pressures below atmospheric; always gauge readings.
Microns of Mercury = 500 micron vacuum is adequate for more refrigerant circuit evacuations.

Manifold Gauge Set
Used for preliminary leak checking, evacuation, charging and refrigerant transfer.
Consists of a pair of gauges and a manifold chamber.
Low pressure gauge on left and blue; high pressure gauge on right and red.
Three sections of manifold chamber: Low side (left), high side (right) and center hose flow control.
Center service hose connected to external equipment needed for specific job (evacuation, charging, recovery, etc.)
Opening hand valve opens chamber to pressure of center chamber. Both valves open all three chambers at same pressure.

BASIC CLEANING PROCEDURES

TABLE OF CONTENTS

		Page
I.	TRASH REMOVAL	1
II.	CLEANING URNS AND ASHTRAYS	3
III.	DUSTING	4
IV.	FLOOR DUSTING	12
V.	VACUUMING (WET, DAMP, SPOT)	14
VI.	MOPPING (WET, DAMP, SPOT)	16

BASIC CLEANING PROCEDURES

I. TRASH REMOVAL

PURPOSE: To remove waste from patient and tenant areas in order to provide the highest standard of sanitation; protection against fire, pests, odor, bacteria, and other health hazards; and for esthetic reasons.

EQUIPMENT:
- Utility cart
- Trash chart
- Bucket
- Germicidal detergent
- Plastic liners (small and large)
- Cloths
- Gloves
- Container for cigarette butts

SAFETY PRECAUTIONS:

1. Must wear gloves.

2. Never handle trash with bare hands.

3. Always empty cigarette butts into separate container that has water or sand in it.

4. If liners are not used, do not transfer trash from one container to another transfer trash into a liner.

5. Trash must be separated into two categories: General and Special, General

PROCEDURE

General

1. Assemble necessary equipment, prepare germicidal solution, and take to assigned area.

2. Put on gloves.

3. Pick up large trash on floor, place in trash container.

4. Close plastic liner and secure with tie.

5. Remove liner and place in trash bag on utility cart or place into trash cart, or other trash collection vehicle.

6. Emerge (dip) cloth into germicidal solution. Wring out thoroughly.

7. Wipe outside and inside of trash container. Dry with second cloth.

8. Replace liner. Liner should extend over top of trash container and fold outward over the upper rim. If plastic liners are not being used, use the Replacement Method—a clean container is exchanged for the dirty one.

9. Proceed with this procedure until all trash is collected or containers are full.

10. Place in utility room or an appropriate storage area until time for disposal.

11. Remove trash from the storage area at the end of the day or at some specified time (by cart or dolly) to dumpsters.

12. If large G.I. cans are used in the specified trash storage area, maintain as listed above.

13. At least once a month, take all trash cans to a specified area and thoroughly wash or steam clean.

14. If using the Replacement Method, dirty trash containers must be washed or steam-cleaned daily. Must be stored in inverted or upside-down position to air dry.

15. Clean all equipment and return to designated storage area. Restock utility cart.

Special Waste Handling Syringes-Hypodermic Needles-Razor Blades

1. Collect from specified areas (full disposable containers designed for this waste.

2. Place in 20-gallon galvanized container in locked designated area.

3. Call Garage for pick-up and disposal when container is full (10).

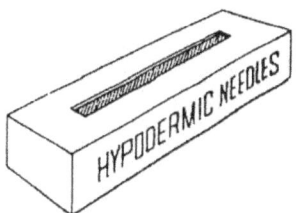

Glass and Aerosol Cans

1. Collect from designated areas in marked metal containers.

2. Place in 20-gallon galvanized containers in locked designated area daily.

3. Call Garage for pick-up and disposal when container is full.

Pathological Specimen (Tissue-flesh)

1. This type of waste is handled by a special technologist in the Hospital's Pathological Division.

2. Must be stored in refrigerator until incinerated.

3. Must be incinerated in special incinerator designed for this purpose.

Contaminated

The same procedure is used as for general collection with the following exceptions:

1. Must have covered step-on containers.

2. A second person is required to hold clean liner (top folded over hands for protection).

3. The tied soiled plastic liner is removed from the waste container and placed in a clean plastic liner and then deposited into the regular trash.

4. If in areas that are restricted, must wear protective garments.

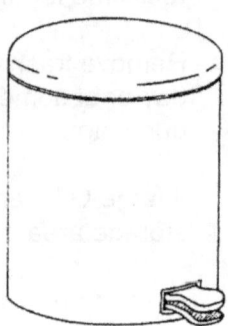

II. CLEANING URNS AND ASHTRAYS

PURPOSE: To prevent fire hazards, to control bacteria, and for appearance.

EQUIPMENT:
    Utility cart
    Sifter or slit spoon
    Bucket for sand
    Cloths or sponges
    Container for cigarette butts
    Gloves
    Buckets (two)
    Counter brush and dustpans
    Germicidal detergent

SAFETY PRECAUTIONS:

1. Wear gloves.

2. Do not place plastic liners on inside of urns.

3. Sweep up all spilled sand immediately.

4. Make sure cigarette butts are placed in special container with water or sand in the bottom.

PROCEDURE

1. Assemble equipment. Prepare solution. Take to designated area.

2. Put on gloves.

3. Empty ashtrays into solution. Wash. Rinse in clear water. Dry. Return to proper area.

4. Make sure cigarette butts are placed in special container with water or sand in the bottom.

    a. Smoke stands and wall urns:

        (1) Empty cigarette butts into special container (by lifting out inside bucket or unscrewing base from top).

        (2) Wash, rinse, and dry the base, top, bucket and wall attachment.

    b. Floor urns with sand:

        (1) Take out large pieces of trash.

(2) Lift screen to remove cigarette butts and any other waste. Use sifter and spoon for this procedure if screens are not in use.

5. Replace sand if necessary. Sweep up any spilled sand.

6. Dip cloth into germicide solution. Wring out. Wipe off rim and outside of urns. Rinse and dry.

7. Continue this procedure until all urns are completed.

8. Clean all equipment and return to designated storage.

9. At least once a month collect cigarette receptacles. Take to utility room. Remove sand where applicable. Submerge in germicidal solution. Wash thoroughly. Rinse and dry. Replace sand and return to designated areas.

III. DUSTING

PURPOSE: To remove accumulated soil, to control bacteria, for protection, and for appearance.

EQUIPMENT:
    Utility cart
    Treated cloths
    Germicidal detergent
    Gloves
    Furniture polish
    Sweeping tool or broom
    Extension handle
    Clean cloths
    Buckets (two)
    Vacuum cleaner (Wet and Dry or Back Pack)
    Broom bags

SAFETY PRECAUTIONS:

1. A fold dust cloth is more efficient than a bunched cloth. When folded properly, cloth may have as many as 32 clean sides.

2. Use treated cloths or damp cloths when dusting. (Never use a feather duster.)

3. Oily cloths are fire hazards; they must be stored in a covered container.

4. Never shake cloth.

5. Never use circular motion. Dust with the grain.

6. Never use excessive water on wood furniture.

7. Do not take dust cloth from one patient unit to the next.

PROCEDURE

General – Dry

1. Assemble equipment. Prepare solution. Take to assigned area.

2. Put on gloves.

3. Fold treated cloth or damp germicidal cloth. (If using the damp germicidal cloth, use a second cloth for polishing.)

4. Look at area. Begin dusting at a point to avoid backtracking. Use both hands whenever possible. Begin with high furniture and work down to low furniture (for example, dust file cabinets before dusting desk tops).

5. Refold cloth when sides become dust filled or refresh by returning to germicidal solution.

6. Continue dusting until area is completed.

7. Inspect work.

8. Clean equipment and return to designated storage area. Cleaning cloths are placed in liner for laundering; woven treated paper dust cloths are discarded.

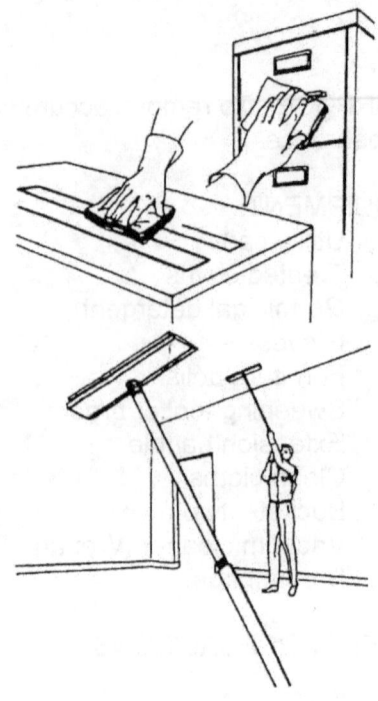

Wall and Ceiling Dusting

1. Assemble equipment. Take to assigned area.

2. Move furniture that will interfere with operation to one side of the room. Remove all pictures and other wall mountings and place in a safe area.

3. Put on gloves.

4. Dust ceiling. Start at back of room. Use vacuum or floor tool or covered broom with extension handle. Place dusting tool against ceiling surface and walk forward to the other end.

5. Turn and overlap stroke. Continue this procedure until completed.

6. Dust ceiling both cross-wise and lengthwise.

7. When ceiling is completed, dust walls from top to bottom. Use full-length vertical overlapping strokes. Include vents, ledges, and exposed pipes.

8. When one side of area is completed, replace furniture.

9. Move furniture from other side and continue the dusting procedure until entire area is completed.

10. Replace furniture, pictures, and other wall mountings.

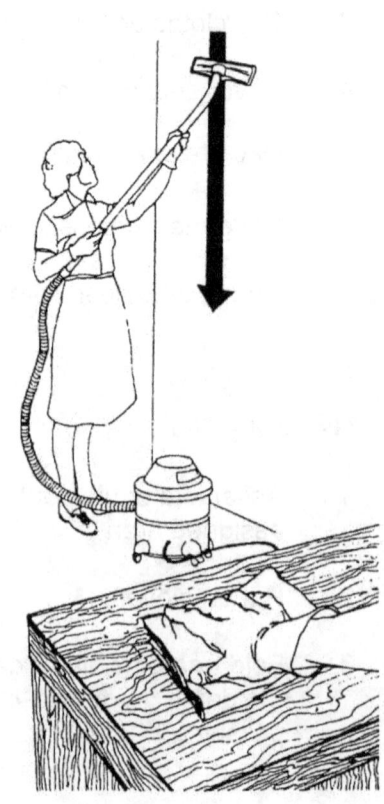

11. Inspect work.

12. Clean equipment. Return to designated storage areas. Broom bags are placed in plastic liner/bag for laundering; woven treated paper dust cloths are discarded.

General Comments for Dusting Different Types of Furniture

1. Wooden Furniture:

   a. Dust entire surface.

   b. Apply polish—pour small amount on damp cloth—rub with grain.

   c. Finish polishing by rubbing with dry cloth.

   d. Surface may be washed with natural detergent.

   CAUTION: Excessive amount of water should be avoided.

2. Metal Furniture:

   a. Dust entire surface.

   b. Surface may be washed and polished.

   c. Apply polish—pour small amount on damp cloth—rub in.

   d. Polish/rub thoroughly with a second cloth.

3. Plastic, Vinyl or Fiberglass:

   a. Dust entire area.

   b. Wash with germicidal cleaning solution.

   c. Rinse.

   d. Rub surface dry.

4. Leather:

   a. Damp dust.

   b. Clean with leather polish or saddle soap.

5. Upholstered Pieces:

   a. Vacuum entire surface thoroughly. Use push-pull strokes.

   b. Lift cushion—vacuum both sides, cushion support, and bottom of chair. Do not overlook corners and crevices.

   c. Check carefully for stains and report to supervisor.

6. Naugahyde:

   a. Elastic:

      (1) Ordinary Dirt: Ordinary dirt can be removed by washing with warm water and a mild soap. Apply soapy water to a large area and allow to soak for a few minutes. This will loosen the dirt. Brisk rubbing with a cloth should then remove most dirt. This procedure may be repeated several times if necessary.

      In the case of stubborn or imbedded dirt in the grain of the Naugahyde, a fingernail brush or other soft bristle brush may be used after the mild soap application has been made.

      If the dirt is extremely difficult to remove, wall washing preparations may be used. Abrasive cleaners may also be used. Abrasive cleaners should be used more cautiously and care exercised to prevent contact with the wood or metal parts of furniture or with any soft fabric which may be a part of the furniture.

      (2) Chewing Gum: Chewing gum may be removed by careful scraping and by applying kerosene, gasoline, or naphtha. If none of these are available, most hair oils or Three-In-One oil will soften the chewing gum so that it may be removed.

      (3) Tars, Asphalts, Creosote: Each of these items will stain Naugahyde if allowed to remain in contact. They should be wiped off

as quickly as possible and the area carefully cleaned with a cloth dampened with kerosene, range oil, gasoline, or naphtha.

(4) Paint: Paint should be removed immediately if possible. Do not use paint remover or liquid-type brush cleaners. An unprinted cloth dampened with kerosene, painter's naphtha or turpentine may be used. Care must be exercised to keep these fluids from contact with soft fabrics or with the wooden areas of the furniture.

(5) Sulphide Staining: Atmosphere permeated with coal gas or direct contact with hard-boiled eggs, "Cold Wave" solutions and other sulphide compounds can stain Naugahyde. These stains may be removed by placing a clean, unprinted piece of cloth over the spotted area and pouring a liberal amount of 6% hydrogen peroxide onto the cloth and allowing the saturated cloth to remain on the spotted area for at least thirty minutes to one hour. If spot is stubborn, allow the hydrogen peroxide saturated cloth to remain on the spotted area overnight. Caution must be used to see that the hydrogen peroxide solution does not come in contact with stained or lacquered wood and should not be allowed to seep into the seams as it will weaken the cotton thread.

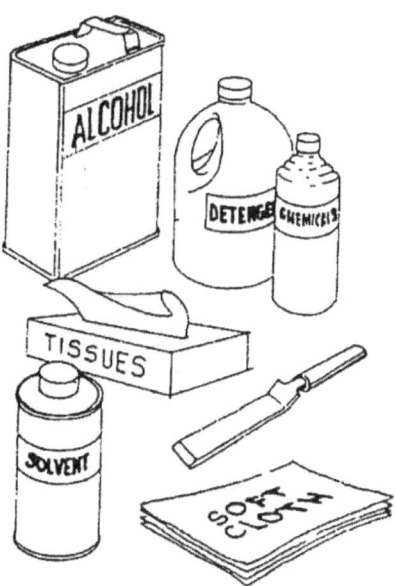

(6) Nail Polish and Nail Polish Remover: These substances will cause permanent harm to Naugahyde on prolonged contact. Fast and careful wiping or blotting immediately after contact will minimize the staining. Spreading of the liquid while removing should be avoided.

(7) Shoe Polish: Most shoe polishes contain dyes which will penetrate the Naugahyde and stain it permanently. They should be wiped off as quickly as possible using kerosene, gasoline, naphtha, or lighter fluid. If staining occurs, the same procedure outlined above for sulphide staining using hydrogen peroxide should be tried.

(8) Shoe Heel Marks: Shoe heel marks can be removed by the same procedure as is recommended for paint.

(9) Ballpoint Ink: Ballpoint ink may sometimes removed if rubbed immediately with a damp cloth using water or rubbing alcohol. If this is not successful, the procedure outlined for sulphide staining may be tried.

(10) Generally, stains are found which do not respond to any of the other treatments. It is sometimes helpful to place the furniture in direct sunlight for two or three days. Mustard, ballpoint ink, certain shoe polishes and dyes will sometimes bleach out in direct sunlight and leave the Naugahyde undamaged.

(11) Waxing or Refinishing: Waxing improves the soil resistance and cleanability of Naugahyde, and any solid wax may be used.

b. Breathable: U.S. Naugaweave should be treated as a soft fabric and not as a fully vinyl-coated fabric. U.S. Naugaweave can be cleaned with foam-type cleansers generally used for soft fabrics.

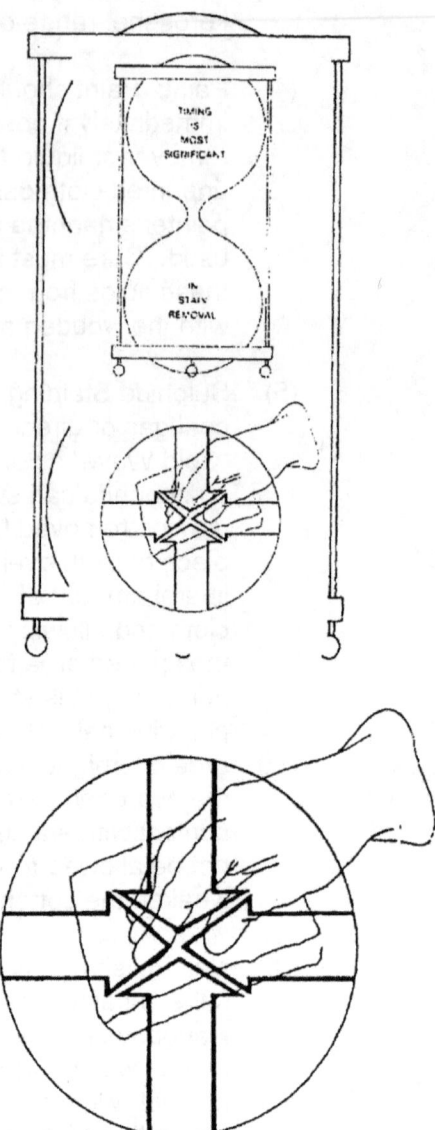

IV. FLOOR DUSTING
(Sweeping/Dusting with Covered Broom or Floor Tool with Chemically Treated Disposal Floor Cloth)

PURPOSE: To remove surface dirt, and make washing easier.

EQUIPMENT:
    Utility cart
    Dustpan
    Treated cloths, or
    Broom bags
    Counter brush
    Sweeping tool, or
    Vacuum cleaner

SAFETY PRECAUTIONS:

1. Never leave piles of dirt and trash in any area.

2. Lift sweeping tool at the end of each stroke. Do not tap.

3. Never put waste or sweepings in a patient's wastebasket.

4. Keep all equipment out of traffic areas.

5. Use of disposable cloths should be limited to two surfaces (i.e., use two treated cloths per ward, and two Administrative units can be cleaned with one cloth).

PROCEDURE

1. Assemble equipment. Take to assigned area.

2. Move furniture, if necessary.

3. Start dusting/sweeping at far end of room or area and work toward door.

4. Place floor tool on direct line with right toe. Hold handle loosely. Stand erect with feet about eight inches apart. Start dusting/sweeping floor-walking forward. Use a push stroke, lift tool at end of each stroke. Do not tap. Overlap each stroke.

5. Continue this procedure until area is completed. Clean under all stationary equipment and furniture.

6. Take up accumulated dirt. Use dustpan and counter brush. Place in plastic liner/trash bag on utility cart.

13

7. The dusting/sweeping procedure can be performed with the wet and dry vacuum cleaner. Dusting Isolation Units must be performed with vacuum.

8. Inspect work. Floor should not have any dust streaks. Replace furniture.

9. Clean equipment. Return to designated storage area. Discard disposable treated cloths. If broom bags are used, place in plastic liner/bag for laundering.

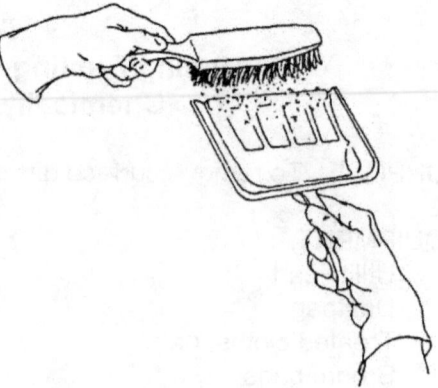

V. VACUUMING
(Wet and Dry)

PURPOSE: To remove dust and dirt and water, to control the spread of bacteria, to aid in reaching difficult-to-reach areas, and for appearance. This operation may be performed on floors, walls, ceiling, rugs, and carpets.

EQUIPMENT:
Upright or tank vacuum cleaner
Wet and dry vacuum cleaner
Attachments: Crevice tool, shelf brush, pipe brush, upholstery brush, walls and ceiling brush, dusting brush, and floor-dry and wet tools.

SAFETY PRECAUTIONS:

1. Empty vacuum when bag is half full.

2. If disposable bag is not in use, empty soil into plastic liner/bag.

3. Never position equipment so that it becomes a tripping hazard.

PROCEDURE

Dry

1. Assemble proper equipment and attachments for the area to be vacuumed:

    a. Upright vacuum for carpet

    b. Tank cleaner to use on floors, grooves, and high cleaning.

    c. Back-pack for stairs, hard to reach areas, walls and ceiling, and drapery.

2. Remove all furniture and other items interfering with the operation.

3. Start in farthest corner of room, area or top of item. Vacuum the surface in a back-and-forth motion.

4. Empty bag when half full. Continue this procedure until area or item is completed. Change attachments as required.

5. Replace furniture or items.

6. Take equipment to utility room. Empty and clean. Return to designated storage area.

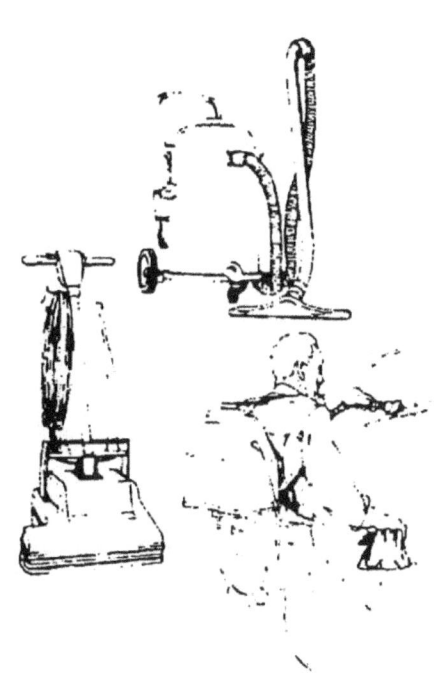

Wet

This procedure is used to remove water. It is considered very effective in the daily performance of different tasks in order to control the spread of infectious organisms. Wet vacuuming is often used in emergencies—flooding, pipe breaks, and overflows. See vacuum cleaning guide under Care of Equipment for operation of the wet vacuum.

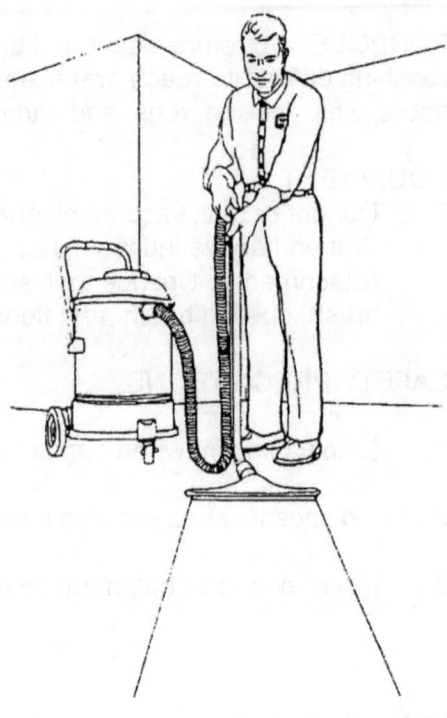

VI. MOPPING
(Wet, Damp, Spot)

PURPOSE: To insure maximum cleanliness, to improve the sanitation of the environment, to aid in control of bacteria, and for the appearance of the area.

EQUIPMENT:
- Utility cart
- Buckets (two)
- Dolly
- Wringers (two)
- Mopheads and handles (two)
- Nylon abrasive pad
- Caution signs
- Gloves
- Broom-Broom bags
- Sweeping tool-treated cloths
- Wet and dry vacuum cleaner
- Putty knife
- Dustpan
- Counter brush
- Germicidal detergent

SAFETY PRECAUTIONS:

1. Sweep or vacuum before mopping.

2. Post area with "Wet Floor" signs.

3. Mop one-half of corridor at a time.

4. Keep equipment close to walls and away from doors and corners.

5. Excessive water should not be allowed to remain on the floor for any length of time because it will cause damage to nearly all types of flooring material.

6. Begin the operation with clean equipment, mopheads, and clean solution.

7. Change cleaning solution and rinse water frequently (every three to four rooms, depending on size and soilage factors).

8. Solution containers should be conveniently positioned so as not to cause tripping or walking over cleaned areas.

PROCEDURE

Wet Mopping

1. Assemble equipment. Fill one container two-thirds full with water. Add recommended amount of germicidal detergent. Fill second container two-thirds full with clear water.

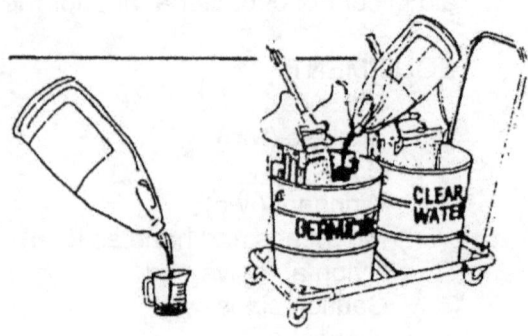

2. Proceed to designated work area. Post "Wet Floor" signs. Move furniture to simplify operation. Vacuum or dust area with covered broom or tool with treated cloth. Remove gum with putty knife. (Use dustpan and counter brush to remove debris and trash.)

3. Dip one mop into cleaning solution and press out excess water to prevent dripping.

4. First, apply solution on and along baseboard or coving. Use the heel of mophead to clean baseboard and corners. (The putty knife can be used to clean out heavily soiled corners or strands of the mophead wrapped around gloved fingertips is another tool for cleaning the corners. A baseboard scrubber or an improvised abrasive pad on a mop handle can be used to remove built-up soil on baseboards.)

5. Return mop to germicidal solution. Churn thoroughly, wring out and pick up solution off baseboards. Apply rinse water with second mop and dry.

6. Continue with the mopping operation. Take solution mop (with excess water pressed out) and make an eight-inch border around floor area approximately nine feet wide and twelve feet long.

7. Begin at top of area. Place mop flat on floor, feet well apart. Place right hand palm up, almost two inches from end of handle, and left hand palm down, about fourteen inches on handle. Begin swinging mop from left to right or right to left using a continuous open figure-eight motion. At the end of approximately six to nine strokes (width of strokes depend on height and weight of worker), turn mop over or renew direction by lapping mop (lift mophead and loop it over the strands). Continue this procedure until area is completed. (A nylon pad attached to one side of mophead can be used to remove black marks while performing the daily mopping procedure.)

8. Return mop to germicidal solution. Churn thoroughly. Wring out and pick up solution. Use same procedure as for applying solution.

9. Dip the second mop into the rinse water, press out excess water, and apply rinse water to area. Use same procedure for rinsing as for applying cleaning solution.

10. Dip the second mop again into rinse water, wring out thoroughly and dry floor using side-to-side stroke.

11. Continue the four steps of mopping, picking up, rinsing, and drying until the area has been covered. Change cleaning solution and rinse water frequently.

12. Inspect work; a properly mopped floor should have a clean surface. There should be no water spots. The corners should be clean and baseboards should not be splashed.

13. Wash and dry equipment and return to designated storage area.

14. Mophead are removed and placed in a plastic bag, and then placed in a regular laundry bag and stored in the designated area to be picked up and laundered.

Damp Mobbing

Damp mopping is a type of mopping used to remove surface dust. This procedure may be used in place of dry dust mopping. Each time mop is dipped into solution or rinse water, it is wrung out thoroughly. The same motions are carried out in this procedure as are for the wet mopping.

Spot Mopping

Spot mopping is a type of mopping used only when a small area is soiled by spillage (water, coke, coffee, urine, and other liquids). Spillage must be wiped up immediately in order to prevent slipping and falling hazards. First, absorb liquid with paper towels or blotters, then mop area.

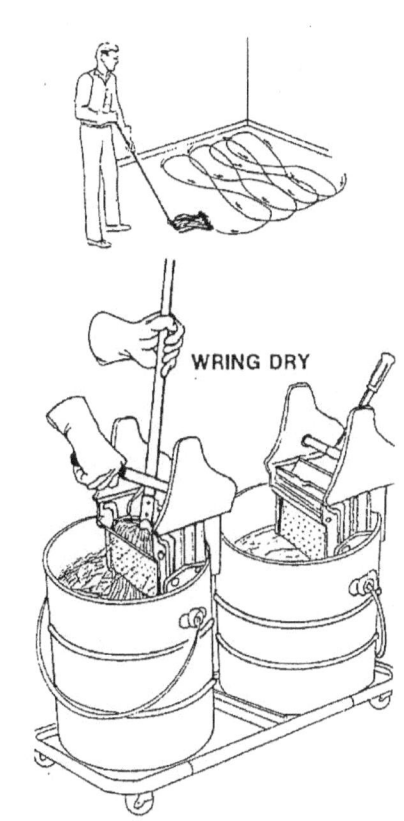

PHILOSOPHY, PRINCIPLES, PRACTICES, AND TECHNICS OF SUPERVISION, ADMINISTRATION, MANAGEMENT, AND ORGANIZATION

TABLE OF CONTENTS

	Page
MEANING OF SUPERVISION	1
THE OLD AND THE NEW SUPERVISION	1
THE EIGHT (8) BASIC PRINCIPLES OF THE NEW SUPERVISION	1
I. Principle of Responsibility	1
II. Principle of Authority	2
III. Principle of Self-Growth	2
IV. Principle of Individual Worth	2
V. Principle of Creative Leadership	2
VI. Principle of Success and Failure	2
VII. Principle of Science	3
VIII. Principle of Cooperation	3
WHAT IS ADMINISTRATION?	3
I. Practices Commonly Classed as "Supervisory"	3
II. Practices Commonly Classed as "Administrative"	3
III. Practices Commonly Classed as Both "Supervisory" and "Administrative"	4
RESPONSIBILITIES OF THE SUPERVISOR	4
COMPETENCIES OF THE SUPERVISOR	4
THE PROFESSIONAL SUPERVISOR-EMPLOYEE RELATIONSHIP	4
MINI-TEXT IN SUPERVISION, ADMINISTRATION, MANAGEMENT, AND ORGANIZATION	5
I. Brief Highlights	5
A. Levels of Management	6
B. What the Supervisor Must Learn	6
C. A Definition of Supervision	6
D. Elements of the Team Concept	6
E. Principles of Organization	6
F. The Four Important Parts of Every Job	7
G. Principles of Delegation	7
H. Principles of Effective Communications	7
I. Principles of Work Improvement	7
J. Areas of Job Improvement	7
K. Seven Key Points in Making Improvements	8

	L.	Corrective Techniques for Job Improvement	8
	M.	A Planning Checklist	8
	N.	Five Characteristics of Good Directions	9
	O.	Types of Directions	9
	P.	Controls	9
	Q.	Orienting the New Employee	9
	R.	Checklist for Orienting New Employees	9
	S.	Principles of Learning	10
	T.	Causes of Poor Performance	10
	U.	Four Major Steps in On-the-Job Instructions	10
	V.	Employees Want Five Things	10
	W.	Some Don'ts in Regard to Praise	11
	X.	How to Gain Your Workers' Confidence	11
	Y.	Sources of Employee Problems	11
	Z.	The Supervisor's Key to Discipline	11
	AA.	Five Important Processes of Management	12
	BB.	When the Supervisor Fails to Plan	12
	CC.	Fourteen General Principles of Management	12
	DD.	Change	12
II.	Brief Topical Summaries		13
	A.	Who/What is the Supervisor?	13
	B.	The Sociology of Work	13
	C.	Principles and Practices of Supervision	14
	D.	Dynamic Leadership	14
	E.	Processes for Solving Problems	15
	F.	Training for Results	15
	G.	Health, Safety, and Accident Prevention	16
	H.	Equal Employment Opportunity	16
	I.	Improving Communications	16
	J.	Self-Development	17
	K.	Teaching and Training	17
		1. The Teaching Process	17
		a. Preparation	17
		b. Presentation	18
		c. Summary	18
		d. Application	18
		e. Evaluation	18
		2. Teaching Methods	18
		a. Lecture	18
		b. Discussion	18
		c. Demonstration	19
		d. Performance	19
		e. Which Method to Use	19

PHILOSOPHY, PRINCIPLES, PRACTICES, AND TECHNICS
OF
SUPERVISION, ADMINISTRATION, MANAGEMENT, AND ORGANIZATION

MEANING OF SUPERVISION

The extension of the democratic philosophy has been accompanied by an extension in the scope of supervision. Modern leaders and supervisors no longer think of supervision in the narrow sense of being confined chiefly to visiting employees, supplying materials, or rating the staff. They regard supervision as being intimately related to all the concerned agencies of society, they speak of the supervisor's function in terms of "growth," rather than the "improvement" of employees.

This modern concept of supervision may be defined as follows: Supervision is leadership and the development of leadership within groups which are cooperatively engaged in inspection, research, training, guidance, and evaluation.

THE OLD AND THE NEW SUPERVISION

TRADITIONAL
1. Inspection
2. Focused on the employee
3. Visitation
4. Random and haphazard
5. Imposed and authoritarian
6. One person usually

MODERN
1. Study and analysis
2. Focused on aims, materials, methods, supervisors, employees, environment
3. Demonstrations, intervisitation, workshops, directed reading, bulletins, etc.
4. Definitely organized and planned (scientific)
5. Cooperative and democratic
6. Many persons involved (creative)

THE EIGHT (8) BASIC PRINCIPLES OF THE NEW SUPERVISION

I. Principle of Responsibility
   Authority to act and responsibility for acting must be joined.
   A. If you give responsibility, give authority.
   B. Define employee duties clearly.
   C. Protect employees from criticism by others.
   D. Recognize the rights as well as obligations of employees.
   E. Achieve the aims of a democratic society insofar as it is possible within the area of your work.
   F. Establish a situation favorable to training and learning.
   G. Accept ultimate responsibility for everything done in your section, unit, office, division, department.
   H. Good administration and good supervision are inseparable.

II. Principle of Authority
The success of the supervisor is measured by the extent to which the power of authority is not used.
   A. Exercise simplicity and informality in supervision
   B. Use the simplest machinery of supervision
   C. If it is good for the organization as a whole, it is probably justified.
   D. Seldom be arbitrary or authoritative.
   E. Do not base your work on the power of position or of personality.
   F. Permit and encourage the free expression of opinions.

III. Principle of Self-Growth
The success of the supervisor is measured by the extent to which, and the speed with which, he is no longer needed.
   A. Base criticism on principles, not on specifics.
   B. Point out higher activities to employees.
   C. Train for self-thinking by employees to meet new situations.
   D. Stimulate initiative, self-reliance, and individual responsibility
   E. Concentrate on stimulating the growth of employees rather than on removing defects.

IV. Principle of Individual Worth
Respect for the individual is a paramount consideration in supervision.
   A. Be human and sympathetic in dealing with employees.
   B. Don't nag about things to be done.
   C. Recognize the individual differences among employees and seek opportunities to permit best expression of each personality.

V. Principle of Creative Leadership
The best supervision is that which is not apparent to the employee.
   A. Stimulate, don't drive employees to creative action.
   B. Emphasize doing good things.
   C. Encourage employees to do what they do best.
   D. Do not be too greatly concerned with details of subject or method.
   E. Do not be concerned exclusively with immediate problems and activities.
   F. Reveal higher activities and make them both desired and maximally possible.
   G. Determine procedures in the light of each situation but see that these are derived from a sound basic philosophy.
   H. Aid, inspire, and lead so as to liberate the creative spirit latent in all good employees.

VI. Principle of Success and Failure
There are no unsuccessful employees, only unsuccessful supervisors who have failed to give proper leadership.
   A. Adapt suggestions to the capacities, attitudes, and prejudices of employees.
   B. Be gradual, be progressive, be persistent.
   C. Help the employee find the general principle; have the employee apply his own problem to the general principle.
   D. Give adequate appreciation for good work and honest effort.
   E. Anticipate employee difficulties and help to prevent them.
   F. Encourage employees to do the desirable things they will do anyway.
   G. Judge your supervision by the results it secures.

VII. Principle of Science
Successful supervision is scientific, objective, and experimental. It is based on facts, not on prejudices.
    A.   Be cumulative in results.
    B.   Never divorce your suggestions from the goals of training.
    C.   Don't be impatient of results.
    D.   Keep all matters on a professional, not a personal, level.
    E.   Do not be concerned exclusively with immediate problems and activities.
    F.   Use objective means of determining achievement and rating where possible.

VIII. Principle of Cooperation
Supervision is a cooperative enterprise between supervisor and employee.
    A.   Begin with conditions as they are.
    B.   Ask opinions of all involved when formulating policies.
    C.   Organization is as good as its weakest link.
    D.   Let employees help to determine policies and department programs.
    E.   Be approachable and accessible—physically and mentally.
    F.   Develop pleasant social relationships.

WHAT IS ADMINISTRATION

Administration is concerned with providing the environment, the material facilities, and the operational procedures that will promote the maximum growth and development of supervisors and employees. (Organization is an aspect and a concomitant of administration.)

There is no sharp line of demarcation between supervision and administration; these functions are intimately interrelated and, often, overlapping. They are complementary activities.

I. Practices Commonly Classed as "Supervisory"
    A.   Conducting employees' conferences
    B.   Visiting sections, units, offices, divisions, departments
    C.   Arranging for demonstrations
    D.   Examining plans
    E.   Suggesting professional reading
    F.   Interpreting bulletins
    G.   Recommending in-service training courses
    H.   Encouraging experimentation
    I.   Appraising employee morale
    J.   Providing for intervisitation

II. Practices Commonly Classified as "Administrative"
    A.   Management of the office
    B.   Arrangement of schedules for extra duties
    C.   Assignment of rooms or areas
    D.   Distribution of supplies
    E.   Keeping records and reports
    F.   Care of audio-visual materials
    G.   Keeping inventory records
    H.   Checking record cards and books

    I. Programming special activities
    J. Checking on the attendance and punctuality of employees

III. Practices Commonly Classified as Both "Supervisory" and "Administrative"
    A. Program construction
    B. Testing or evaluating outcomes
    C. Personnel accounting
    D. Ordering instructional materials

RESPONSIBILITIES OF THE SUPERVISOR

A person employed in a supervisory capacity must constantly be able to improve his own efficiency and ability. He represent the employer to the employees and only continuous self-examination can make him a capable supervisor.

Leadership and training are the supervisor's responsibility. An efficient working unit is one in which the employees work with the supervisor. It is his job to bring out the best in his employees. He must always be relaxed, courteous, and calm in his association with his employees. Their feelings are important, and a harsh attitude does not develop the most efficient employees.

COMPETENCES OF THE SUPERVISOR

    I.   Complete knowledge of the duties and responsibilities of his position.
    II.   To be able to organize a job, plan ahead, and carry through.
    III. To have self-confidence and initiative.
    IV.   To be able to handle the unexpected situation and make quick decisions.
    V.   To be able to properly train subordinates in the positions they are best suited for.
    VI.   To be able to keep good human relations among his subordinates.
    VII. To be able to keep good human relations between his subordinates and himself and to earn their respect and trust.

THE PROFESSIONAL SUPERVISOR-EMPLOYEE RELATIONSHIP

There are two kinds of efficiency: one kind is only apparent and is produced in organizations through the exercise of mere discipline; this is but a simulation of the second, or true, efficiency which springs from spontaneous cooperation. If you are a manager, no matter how great or small your responsibility, it is your job, in the final analysis, to create and develop this involuntary cooperation among the people whom you supervise. For, no matter how powerful a combination of money, machines, and materials a company may have, this is a dead and sterile thing without a team of willing, thinking, and articulate people to guide it.

The following 21 points are presented as indicative of the exemplary basic relationship that should exist between supervisor and employee:

1. Each person wants to be liked and respected by his fellow employee and wants to be treated with consideration and respect by his superior.
2. The most competent employee will make an error. However, in a unit where good relations exist between the supervisor and his employees, tenseness and fear do not exist. Thus, errors are not hidden or covered up, and the efficiency of a unit is not impaired.

3. Subordinates resent rules, regulations, or orders that are unreasonable or unexplained.
4. Subordinates are quick to resent unfairness, harshness, injustices, and favoritism.
5. An employee will accept responsibility if he knows that he will be complimented for a job well done, and not too harshly chastised for failure; that his supervisor will check the cause of the failure, and, if it was the supervisor's fault, he will assume the blame therefore. If it was the employee's fault, his supervisor will explain the correct method or means of handling the responsibility.
6. An employee wants to receive credit for a suggestion he has made, that is used. If a suggestion cannot be used, the employee is entitled to an explanation. The supervisor should not say "no" and close the subject.
7. Fear and worry slow up a worker's ability. Poor working environment can impair his physical and mental health. A good supervisor avoids forceful methods, threats, and arguments to get a job done.
8. A forceful supervisor is able to train his employees individually and as a team, and is able to motivate them in the proper channels.
9. A mature supervisor is able to properly evaluate his subordinates and to keep them happy and satisfied.
10. A sensitive supervisor will never patronize his subordinates.
11. A worthy supervisor will respect his employees' confidences.
12. Definite and clear-cut responsibilities should be assigned to each executive.
13. Responsibility should always be coupled with corresponding authority.
14. No change should be made in the scope or responsibilities of a position without a definite understanding to that effect on the part of all persons concerned.
15. No executive or employee, occupying a single position in the organization, should be subject to definite orders from more than one source.
16. Orders should never be given to subordinates over the head of a responsible executive. Rather than do this, the officer in question should be supplanted.
17. Criticisms of subordinates should, whoever possible, be made privately, and in no case should a subordinate be criticized in the presence of executives or employees of equal or lower rank.
18. No dispute or difference between executives or employees as to authority or responsibilities should be considered too trivial for prompt and careful adjudication.
19. Promotions, wage changes, and disciplinary action should always be approved by the executive immediately superior to the one directly responsible.
20. No executive or employee should ever be required, or expected, to be at the same time an assistant to, and critic of, another.
21. Any executive whose work is subject to regular inspection should, wherever practicable, be given the assistance and facilities necessary to enable him to maintain an independent check of the quality of his work.

MINI-TEXT IN SUPERVISION, ADMINISTRATION, MANAGEMENT, AND ORGANIZATION

I. Brief Highlights

Listed concisely and sequentially are major headings and important data in the field for quick recall and review.

A. Levels of Management
Any organization of some size has several levels of management. In terms of a ladder, the levels are:

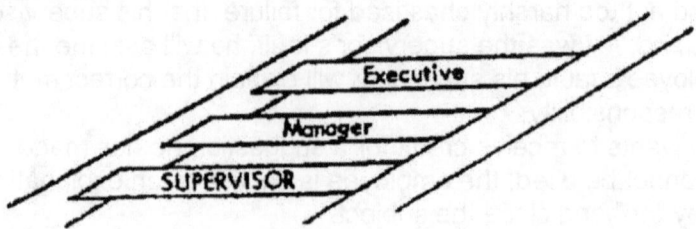

The first level is very important because it is the beginning point of management leadership.

B. What the Supervisor Must Learn
A supervisor must learn to:
1. Deal with people and their differences
2. Get the job done through people
3. Recognize the problems when they exist
4. Overcome obstacles to good performance
5. Evaluate the performance of people
6. Check his own performance in terms of accomplishment

C. A Definition of Supervisor
The term supervisor means any individual having authority, in the interests of the employer, to hire, transfer, suspend, lay-off, recall, promote, discharge, assign, reward, or discipline other employees or responsibility to direct them, or to adjust their grievances, or effectively to recommend such action, if, in connection with the foregoing, exercise of such authority is not of a merely routine or clerical nature but requires the use of independent judgment.

D. Elements of the Team Concept
What is involved in teamwork? The component parts are:
1. Members
2. A leader
3. Goals
4. Plans
5. Cooperation
6. Spirit

E. Principles of Organization
1. A team member must know what his job is.
2. Be sure that the nature and scope of a job are understood.
3. Authority and responsibility should be carefully spelled out.
4. A supervisor should be permitted to make the maximum number of decisions affecting his employees.
5. Employees should report to only one supervisor.
6. A supervisor should direct only as many employees as he can handle effectively.
7. An organization plan should be flexible.

8. Inspection and performance of work should be separate.
9. Organizational problems should receive immediate attention.
10. Assign work in line with ability and experience.

F. The Four Important Parts of Every Job
1. Inherent in every job is the *accountability* for results.
2. A second set of factors in every job is *responsibilities*.
3. Along with duties and responsibilities one must have the *authority* to act within certain limits without obtaining permission to proceed.
4. No job exists in a vacuum. The supervisor is surrounded by key *relationships*.

G. Principles of Delegation
Where work is delegated for the first time, the supervisor should think in terms of these questions:
1. Who is best qualified to do this?
2. Can an employee improve his abilities by doing this?
3. How long should an employee spend on this?
4. Are there any special problems for which he will need guidance?
5. How broad a delegation can I make?

H. Principles of Effective Communications
1. Determine the media.
2. To whom directed?
3. Identification and source authority.
4. Is communication understood?

I. Principles of Work Improvement
1. Most people usually do only the work which is assigned to them.
2. Workers are likely to fit assigned work into the time available to perform it.
3. A good workload usually stimulates output.
4. People usually do their best work when they know that results will be reviewed or inspected.
5. Employees usually feel that someone else is responsible for conditions of work, workplace layout, job methods, type of tools/equipment, and other such factors.
6. Employees are usually defensive about their job security.
7. Employees have natural resistance to change.
8. Employees can support or destroy a supervisor.
9. A supervisor usually earns the respect of his people through his personal example of diligence and efficiency.

J. Areas of Job Improvement
The areas of job improvement are quite numerous, but the most common ones which a supervisor can identify and utilize are:
1. Departmental layout
2. Flow of work
3. Workplace layout
4. Utilization of manpower
5. Work methods
6. Materials handling

7. Utilization
8. Motion economy

K. Seven Key Points in Making Improvements
   1. Select the job to be improved
   2. Study how it is being done now
   3. Question the present method
   4. Determine actions to be taken
   5. Chart proposed method
   6. Get approval and apply
   7. Solicit worker participation

I. Corrective Techniques of Job Improvement
   Specific Problems
   1. Size of workload
   2. Inability to meet schedules
   3. Strain and fatigue
   4. Improper use of men and skills
   5. Waste, poor quality, unsafe conditions
   6. Bottleneck conditions that hinder output
   7. Poor utilization of equipment and machine
   8. Efficiency and productivity of labor

   General Improvement
   1. Departmental layout
   2. Flow of work
   3. Work plan layout
   4. Utilization of manpower
   5. Work methods
   6. Materials handling
   7. Utilization of equipment
   8. Motion economy

   Corrective Techniques
   1. Study with scale model
   2. Flow chart study
   3. Motion analysis
   4. Comparison of units produced to standard allowance
   5. Methods analysis
   6. Flow chart and equipment study
   7. Down time vs. running time
   8. Motion analysis

M. A Planning Checklist
   1. Objectives
   2. Controls
   3. Delegations
   4. Communications
   5. Resources
   6. Manpower

7. Equipment
8. Supplies and materials
9. Utilization of time
10. Safety
11. Money
12. Work
13. Timing of improvements

N. Five Characteristics of Good Directions
In order to get results, directions must be:
1. Possible of accomplishment
2. Agreeable with worker interests
3. Related to mission
4. Planned and complete
5. Unmistakably clear

O. Types of Directions
1. Demands or direct orders
2. Requests
3. Suggestion or implication
4. volunteering

P. Controls
A typical listing of the overall areas in which the supervisor should establish controls might be:
1. Manpower
2. Materials
3. Quality of work
4. Quantity of work
5. Time
6. Space
7. Money
8. Methods

Q. Orienting the New Employee
1. Prepare for him
2. Welcome the new employee
3. Orientation for the job
4. Follow-up

R. Checklist for Orienting New Employees   Yes   No
1. Do you appreciate the feelings of new employees when they first report for work?   ___   ___
2. Are you aware of the fact that the new employee must make a big adjustment to his job?   ___   ___
3. Have you given him good reasons for liking the job and the organization?   ___   ___
4. Have you prepared for his first day on the job?   ___   ___
5. Did you welcome him cordially and make him feel needed?   ___   ___

	Yes	No

6. Did you establish rapport with him so that he feels free to talk and discuss matters with you? ___ ___
7. Did you explain his job to him and his relationship to you? ___ ___
8. Does he know that his work will be evaluated periodically on a basis that is fair and objective? ___ ___
9. Did you introduce him to his fellow workers in such a way that they are likely to accept him? ___ ___
10. Does he know what employee benefits he will receive? ___ ___
11. Does he understand the importance of being on the job and what to do if he must leave his duty station? ___ ___
12. Has he been impressed with the importance of accident prevention and safe practice? ___ ___
13. Does he generally know his way around the department? ___ ___
14. Is he under the guidance of a sponsor who will teach the right way of doing things? ___ ___
15. Do you plan to follow-up so that he will continue to adjust successfully to his job? ___ ___

S. Principles of Learning
   1. Motivation
   2. Demonstration or explanation
   3. Practice

T. Causes of Poor Performance
   1. Improper training for job
   2. Wrong tools
   3. Inadequate directions
   4. Lack of supervisory follow-up
   5. Poor communications
   6. Lack of standards of performance
   7. Wrong work habits
   8. Low morale
   9. Other

U. Four Major Steps in On-The-Job Instruction
   1. Prepare the worker
   2. Present the operation
   3. Tryout performance
   4. Follow-up

V. Employees Want Five Things
   1. Security
   2. Opportunity
   3. Recognition
   4. Inclusion
   5. Expression

W. Some Don'ts in Regard to Praise
   1. Don't praise a person for something he hasn't done.
   2. Don't praise a person unless you can be sincere.
   3. Don't be sparing in praise just because your superior withholds it from you.
   4. Don't let too much time elapse between good performance and recognition of it

X. How to Gain Your Workers' Confidence
   Methods of developing confidence include such things as:
   1. Knowing the interests, habits, hobbies of employees
   2. Admitting your own inadequacies
   3. Sharing and telling of confidence in others
   4. Supporting people when they are in trouble
   5. Delegating matters that can be well handled
   6. Being frank and straightforward about problems and working conditions
   7. Encouraging others to bring their problems to you
   8. Taking action on problems which impede worker progress

Y. Sources of Employee Problems
   On-the-job causes might be such things as:
   1. A feeling that favoritism is exercised in assignments
   2. Assignment of overtime
   3. An undue amount of supervision
   4. Changing methods or systems
   5. Stealing of ideas or trade secrets
   6. Lack of interest in job
   7. Threat of reduction in force
   8. Ignorance or lack of communications
   9. Poor equipment
   10. Lack of knowing how supervisor feels toward employee
   11. Shift assignments

   Off-the-job problems might have to do with:
   1. Health
   2. Finances
   3. Housing
   4. Family

Z. The Supervisor's Key to Discipline
   There are several key points about discipline which the supervisor should keep in mind:
   1. Job discipline is one of the disciplines of life and is directed by the supervisor.
   2. It is more important to correct an employee fault than to fix blame for it.
   3. Employee performance is affected by problems both on the job and off.
   4. Sudden or abrupt changes in behavior can be indications of important employee problems.
   5. Problems should be dealt with as soon as possible after they are identified.
   6. The attitude of the supervisor may have more to do with solving problems than the techniques of problem solving.
   7. Correction of employee behavior should be resorted to only after the supervisor is sure that training or counseling will not be helpful.

8. Be sure to document your disciplinary actions.
9. Make sure that you are disciplining on the basis of facts rather than personal feelings.
10. Take each disciplinary step in order, being careful not to make snap judgments, or decisions based on impatience.

AA. Five Important Processes of Management
1. Planning
2. Organizing
3. Scheduling
4. Controlling
5. Motivating

BB. When the Supervisor Fails to Plan
1. Supervisor creates impression of not knowing his job
2. May lead to excessive overtime
3. Job runs itself—supervisor lacks control
4. Deadlines and appointments missed
5. Parts of the work go undone
6. Work interrupted by emergencies
7. Sets a bad example
8. Uneven workload creates peaks and valleys
9. Too much time on minor details at expense of more important tasks

CC. Fourteen General Principles of Management
1. Division of work
2. Authority and responsibility
3. Discipline
4. Unity of command
5. Unity of direction
6. Subordination of individual interest to general interest
7. Remuneration of personnel
8. Centralization
9. Scalar chain
10. Order
11. Equity
12. Stability of tenure of personnel
13. Initiative
14. Esprit de corps

DD. Change

Bringing about change is perhaps attempted more often, and yet less well understood, than anything else the supervisor does. How do people generally react to change? (People tend to resist change that is imposed upon them by other individuals or circumstances.

Change is characteristic of every situation. It is a part of every real endeavor where the efforts of people are concerned.

1. Why do people resist change?
   People may resist change because of:
   a. Fear of the unknown
   b. Implied criticism
   c. Unpleasant experiences in the past
   d. Fear of loss of status
   e. Threat to the ego
   f. Fear of loss of economic stability

2. How can we best overcome the resistance to change?
   In initiating change, take these steps:
   a. Get ready to sell
   b. Identify sources of help
   c. Anticipate objections
   d. Sell benefits
   e. Listen in depth
   f. Follow up

II. Brief Topical Summaries

   A. Who/What is the Supervisor?
      1. The supervisor is often called the "highest level employee and the lowest level manager."
      2. A supervisor is a member of both management and the work group. He acts as a bridge between the two.
      3. Most problems in supervision are in the area of human relations, or people problems.
      4. Employees expect: Respect, opportunity to learn and to advance, and a sense of belonging, and so forth.
      5. Supervisors are responsible for directing people and organizing work. Planning is of paramount importance.
      6. A position description is a set of duties and responsibilities inherent to a given position.
      7. It is important to keep the position description up-to-date and to provide each employee with his own copy.

   B. The Sociology of Work
      1. People are alike in many ways; however, each individual is unique.
      2. The supervisor is challenged in getting to know employee differences. Acquiring skills in evaluating individuals is an asset.
      3. Maintaining meaningful working relationships in the organization is of great importance.
      4. The supervisor has an obligation to help individuals to develop to their fullest potential.
      5. Job rotation on a planned basis helps to build versatility and to maintain interest and enthusiasm in work groups.
      6. Cross training (job rotation) provides backup skills.

7. The supervisor can help reduce tension by maintaining a sense of humor, providing guidance to employees, and by making reasonable and timely decisions. Employees respond favorably to working under reasonably predictable circumstances.
8. Change is characteristic of all managerial behavior. The supervisor must adjust to changes in procedures, new methods, technological changes, and to a number of new and sometimes challenging situations.
9. To overcome the natural tendency for people to resist change, the supervisor should become more skillful in initiating change.

C. Principles and Practices of Supervision
1. Employees should be required to answer to only one superior.
2. A supervisor can effectively direct only a limited number of employees, depending upon the complexity, variety, and proximity of the jobs involved.
3. The organizational chart presents the organization in graphic form. It reflects lines of authority and responsibility as well as interrelationships of units within the organization.
4. Distribution of work can be improved through an analysis using the "Work Distribution Chart."
5. The "Work Distribution Chart" reflects the division of work within a unit in understandable form.
6. When related tasks are given to an employee, he has a better chance of increasing his skills through training.
7. The individual who is given the responsibility for tasks must also be given the appropriate authority to insure adequate results.
8. The supervisor should delegate repetitive, routine work. Preparation of recurring reports, maintaining leave and attendance records are some examples.
9. Good discipline is essential to good task performance. Discipline is reflected in the actions of employees on the job in the absence of supervision.
10. Disciplinary action may have to be taken when the positive aspects of discipline have failed. Reprimand, warning, and suspension are examples of disciplinary action.
11. If a situation calls for a reprimand, be sure it is deserved and remember it is to be done in private.

D. Dynamic Leadership
1. A style is a personal method or manner of exerting influence.
2. Authoritarian leaders often see themselves as the source of power and authority.
3. The democratic leader often perceives the group as the source of authority and power.
4. Supervisors tend to do better when using the pattern of leadership that is most natural for them.
5. Social scientists suggest that the effective supervisor use the leadership style that best fits the problem or circumstances involved.
6. All four styles—telling, selling, consulting, joining—have their place. Using one does not preclude using the other at another time.

7. The theory X point of view assumes that the average person dislikes work, will avoid it whenever possible, and must be coerced to achieve organizational objectives.
8. The theory Y point of view assumes that the average person considers work to be a natural as play, and, when the individual is committed, he requires little supervision or direction to accomplish desired objectives.
9. The leader's basic assumptions concerning human behavior and human nature affect his actions, decisions, and other managerial practices.
10. Dissatisfaction among employees is often present, but difficult to isolate. The supervisor should seek to weaken dissatisfaction by keeping promises, being sincere and considerate, keeping employees informed, and so forth.
11. Constructive suggestions should be encouraged during the natural progress of the work.

E. Processes for Solving Problems
1. People find their daily tasks more meaningful and satisfying when they can improve them.
2. The causes of problems, or the key factors, are often hidden in the background. Ability to solve problems often involves the ability to isolate them from their backgrounds. There is some substance to the cliché that some persons "can't see the forest for the trees."
3. New procedures are often developed from old ones. Problems should be broken down into manageable parts. New ideas can be adapted from old one.
4. People think differently in problem-solving situations. Using a logical, patterned approach is often useful. One approach found to be useful includes these steps:
   a. Define the problem
   b. Establish objectives
   c. Get the facts
   d. Weigh and decide
   e. Take action
   f. Evaluate action

F. Training for Results
1. Participants respond best when they feel training is important to them.
2. The supervisor has responsibility for the training and development of those who report to him.
3. When training is delegated to others, great care must be exercised to insure the trainer has knowledge, aptitude, and interest for his work as a trainer.
4. Training (learning) of some type goes on continually. The most successful supervisor makes certain the learning contributes in a productive manner to operational goals.
5. New employees are particularly susceptible to training. Older employees facing new job situations require specific training, as well as having need for development and growth opportunities.
6. Training needs require continuous monitoring.
7. The training officer of an agency is a professional with a responsibility to assist supervisors in solving training problems.

8. Many of the self-development steps important to the supervisor's own growth are equally important to the development of peers and subordinates. Knowledge of these is important when the supervisor consults with others on development and growth opportunities.

G. Health, Safety, and Accident Prevention
1. Management-minded supervisors take appropriate measures to assist employees in maintaining health and in assuring safe practices in the work environment.
2. Effective safety training and practices help to avoid injury and accidents.
3. Safety should be a management goal. All infractions of safety which are observed should be corrected without exception.
4. Employees' safety attitude, training and instruction, provision of safe tools and equipment, supervision, and leadership are considered highly important factors which contribute to safety and which can be influenced directly by supervisors.
5. When accidents do occur, they should be investigated promptly for very important reasons, including the fact that information which is gained can be used to prevent accidents in the future.

H. Equal Employment Opportunity
1. The supervisor should endeavor to treat all employees fairly, without regard to religion, race, sex, or national origin.
2. Groups tend to reflect the attitude of the leader. Prejudice can be detected even in very subtle form. Supervisors must strive to create a feeling of mutual respect and confidence in every employee.
3. Complete utilization of all human resources is a national goal. Equitable consideration should be accorded women in the work force, minority-group members, the physically and mentally handicapped, and the older employee. The important question is: "Who can do the job?"
4. Training opportunities, recognition for performance, overtime assignments, promotional opportunities, and all other personnel actions are to be handled on an equitable basis.

I. Improving Communications
1. Communications is achieving understanding between the sender and the receiver of a message. It also means sharing information—the creation of understanding.
2. Communication is basic to all human activity. Words are means of conveying meanings; however, real meanings are in people.
3. There are very practical differences in the effectiveness of one-way, impersonal, and two-way communications. Words spoken face-to-face are better understood. Telephone conversations are effective, but lack the rapport of person-to-person exchanges. The whole person communicates.
4. Cooperation and communication in an organization go hand in hand. When there is a mutual respect between people, spelling out rules and procedures for communicating is unnecessary.
5. There are several barriers to effective communications. These include failure to listen with respect and understanding, lack of skill in feedback, and misinterpreting the meanings of words used by the speaker. It is also common

practice to listen to what we want to hear, and tune out things we do not want to hear.
6. Communication is management's chief problem. The supervisor should accept the challenge to communicate more effectively and to improve interagency and intra-agency communications.
7. The supervisor may often plan for and conduct meetings. The planning phase is critical and may determine the success or the failure of a meeting.
8. Speaking before groups usually requires extra effort. Stage fright may never disappear completely, but it can be controlled.

J. Self-Development
1. Every employee is responsible for his own self-development.
2. Toastmaster and toastmistress clubs offer opportunities to improve skills in oral communications.
3. Planning for one's own self-development is of vital importance. Supervisors know their own strengths and limitations better than anyone else.
4. Many opportunities are open to aid the supervisor in his developmental efforts, including job assignments; training opportunities, both governmental and non-governmental—to include universities and professional conferences and seminars.
5. Programmed instruction offers a means of studying at one's own rate.
6. Where difficulties may arise from a supervisor's being away from his work for training, he may participate in televised home study or correspondence courses to meet his self-development needs.

K. Teaching and Training
1. The Teaching Process
Teaching is encouraging and guiding the learning activities of students toward established goals. In most cases this process consists of five steps: preparation, presentation, summarization, evaluation, and application.

   a. Preparation
   Preparation is two-fold in nature; that of the supervisor and the employee. Preparation by the supervisor is absolutely essential to success. He must know what, when, where, how, and whom he will teach. Some of the factors that should be considered are:
   1) The objectives
   2) The materials needed
   3) The methods to be used
   4) Employee participation
   5) Employee interest
   6) Training aids
   7) Evaluation
   8) Summarization

   Employee preparation consists in preparing the employee to receive the material. Probably the most important single factor in the preparation of the employee is arousing and maintaining his interest. He must know the objectives of the training, why he is there, how the material can be used, and its importance to him.

b. Presentation
In presentation, have a carefully designed plan and follow it. The plan should be accurate and complete, yet flexible enough to meet situations as they arise. The method of presentation will be determined by the particular situation and objectives.

c. Summary
A summary should be made at the end of every training unit and program. In addition, there may be internal summaries depending on the nature of the material being taught. The important thing is that the trainee must always be able to understand how each part of the new material relates to the whole.

d. Application
The supervisor must arrange work so the employee will be given a chance to apply new knowledge or skills while the material is still clear in his mind and interest is high. The trainee does not really know whether he has learned the material until he has been given a chance to apply it. If the material is not applied, it loses most of its value.

e. Evaluation
The purpose of all training is to promote learning. To determine whether the training has been a success or failure, the supervisor must evaluate this learning.
In the broadest sense, evaluation includes all the devices, methods, skills, and techniques used by the supervisor to keep himself and the employees informed as to their progress toward the objectives they are pursuing. The extent to which the employee has mastered the knowledge, skills, and abilities, or changed his attitudes, as determined by the program objectives, is the extent to which instruction has succeeded or failed.
Evaluation should not be confined to the end of the lesson, day, or program but should be used continuously. We shall note later the way this relates to the rest of the teaching process.

2. Teaching Methods
A teaching method is a pattern of identifiable student and instructor activity used in presenting training material.
All supervisors are faced with the problem of deciding which method should be used at a given time.

a. Lecture
The lecture is direct oral presentation of material by the supervisor. The present trend is to place less emphasis on the trainer's activity and more on that of the trainee.

b. Discussion
Teaching by discussion or conference involves using questions and other techniques to arouse interest and focus attention upon certain areas, and by doing so creating a learning situation. This can be one of the most

valuable methods because it gives the employees an opportunity to express their ideas and pool their knowledge.

    c. Demonstration

    The demonstration is used to teach how something works or how to do something. It can be used to show a principle or what the results of a series of actions will be. A well-staged demonstration is particularly effective because it shows proper methods of performance in a realistic manner.

    d. Performance

    Performance is one of the most fundamental of all learning techniques or teaching methods. The trainee may be able to tell how a specific operation should be performed but he cannot be sure he knows how to perform the operation until he has done so.

    As with all methods, there are certain advantages and disadvantages to each method.

    e. Which Method to Use

    Moreover, there are other methods and techniques of teaching. It is difficult to use any method without other methods entering into it. In any learning situation, a combination of methods is usually more effective than any one method alone.

Finally, evaluation must be integrated into the other aspects of the teaching-learning process.

It must be used in the motivation of the trainees; it must be used to assist in developing understanding during the training; and it must be related to employee application of the results of training.

This is distinctly the role of the supervisor.

www.ingramcontent.com/pod-product-compliance
Lightning Source LLC
Chambersburg PA
LVW081819300426
816CB00014B/2419